Arno Ritter
Roderick Ritter

IN SEARCH OF
THE SECRET
OF SUCCESS

BE SUCCESSFUL SUCCESSFULLY IN
BUSINESS AND MANAGEMENT

Imprint

Bibliographic information of the German National Library: The German National Library lists this publication in the Deutsche Nationalbibliografie; detailed bibliographic data are available on the Internet at http://dnb.dnb.de.
Cover and graphical design: Aurelia Ritter
Figures and photos (unless otherwise indicated): Arno Ritter and Aurelia Ritter
Editorial office: Arno Ritter and Aurelia Ritter
© 2024 Arno Ritter and Roderick Ritter
Publisher: BoD • Books on Demand GmbH, In de Tarpen 42, 22848 Norderstedt
Print: Libri Plureos GmbH, Friedensallee 273, 22763 Hamburg
ISBN 978-3-7597-8438-4

Foreword

Success is a topic we have been dealing with for as long as we can remember. We – and you, we assume – have intuitively done a lot of things right, especially, since we recognized some of our success factors confirmed in real life situations. However, there is always something more to learn. Hence, why we cannot avoid a more or less scientific examination of the subject of success. In 2021, we began writing a business novel about "success" inspired somewhat by the movie comedy "The Secret of My Succe$s" starring Michael J. Fox (1987). During our analysis and writing progress, we then also decided to create a short management summary in English, as we are also aware that many people do not have enough time to even read a bulky volume. We present you a short excerpt and some key points from our main book on success (Ritter 2022). We will address questions like "What constitutes success, what contributes to success, or how do we become successful? And then how do we stay successful?" In a nutshell: **how to be successful successfully?** Our focus here is on business and management.

It goes without saying that there cannot be only one opinion or answer to the same question. Moreover, there is an almost unmanageable abundance of ideas, theories, solutions, publications and convictions on the subject of success – for centuries already. As authors, we have therefore made a selective choice and decided to include some of the old masters we consider to be essential, such as Sunzi, Musashi, Machiavelli, Clausewitz, Moltke or Emperor Marcus Aurelius, "management gurus" like Peter Drucker, Jim Collins, Robert Grant, Henry Mintzberg, Gary Hamel and C. K. Prahalad, coaches and consultants like Stephen Covey, Gay Hendricks or Mahan Khalsa, historians like Jörg Nagler or Yuval Noah Harari, scientists like Victor Frankl, authors like Douglas and Scott Adams, Wolfgang Schur and Günter Weick, Daniel Pink, Harro von Senger and many others. Furthermore, we will share our own insights, concepts and approaches for success. We will touch on a wide variety of areas and fields. Therefore, let us dive into evolution and human history, into topics such as personal and corporate success, leadership, innovation, entrepreneurship, career, strategic success, dealing with stratagems (i.e., lists) and implementation. We have tried – whenever possible – to quote the English originals; some of our sources were available to us in German translation or in the German original. In these cases, we either tried to find English translations or we translated the texts ourselves and with the help of Aurelia.

Since we want to focus on the essentials in this book, we do not share details. Moreover, we don't view success as a mathematical science (probability does). Henry Mintzberg rightly points out that there is not one best organization or way to define a strategy (successfully). Look at the ideas for success presented in this book like you would look at a buffet: choose what is best for you! Interestingly enough, this book is an experiment for us, as we wrote it as father and son, with the goal of trying out some of the ideas right away as part of our book project and in everyday life. We hope you enjoy reading it and discover some useful ideas. We would like to thank all our family members, especially Aurelia (our designer, editor and translator), friends, study and business colleagues and customer partners for the many interesting discussions and support, without whom this work would not have been possible.

Arno Ritter and Roderick Ritter (management.kompass@gmx.de)

In memory of Oma Henny and Sandrine

TABLE OF CONTENTS

I

List of Abbreviations

aka	also known as
BANWAD	Beyond Agile, New Work And Digitalization (our concept to meet the challenges of the future, see Glossary and Ritter 2021)
B.C.	Before Christ
BCI	Business Concept Innovation(s)
BHAG	Big Hairy Audacious Goals (see Collins and Porras 2004 and Collins 2020)
CEO	Chief Executive Officer
cf	Confer
DevOps	Integrated process improvement approach for software development, operations and quality
GmbH	Gesellschaft mit beschränkter Haftung (i.e., limited liability company / private limited company)
HMS	His or Her Majesty's Ship
HR(M)	Human Resources (Management)
IQ	Intelligence quotient
IT	Information Technology
KPI	Key Performance Indicator
MBA	Master of Business Administration
MES	Manufacturing Execution System(s)
N/A	Not applicable
No.	Number
NPV	Net Present Value (accounting method, see Glossary)
OECD	Organisation for Economic Co-operation and Development
ORDER	Opportunity, Resources, Decision Process, Exact Solution, Relationship (i.e., a consulting principle according to Khalsa)
PEST	Political, Economic, Social & Technological factors analysis

PESTEL	Analysis of Political, Economic, Social, Technological, Ecological / Environmental and Legal Factors (i.e., an extension of PEST)
PISA	Programme for International Student Assessment
R&D	Research and Development
SMART	Specific – Measurable – Accepted – Realistic – Timely (goals)
Stra-Wach	Strategemische Wachsamkeit (i.e., stratagemic vigilance, see Senger 2016a)
SWOT	Strengths, Weaknesses, Opportunities and Threats (analysis)
TPS	Toyota Production System
TQM	Total Quality Management
TUDAPOL	Think Unlimited, Develop Agile, Produce and Operate Lean (our holistic principle for innovation, development and operation, see pages 110-112 and Ritter 2020)
US / U.S.	The United States
VDI	Verein Deutscher Ingenieure (i.e., The Association of German Engineers)
VIP	Very important person
3D	Three-dimensional
4 Ps	Marketing-Mix: Product, Price, Promotion, Place (see also 7 Ps)
5 Ss	Seiri (Sifting) / Seiton (Sorting) / Seiso (Sweeping clean) / Seiketsu (Spic and Span) / Shitsuke (Sustain); i.e., a (Japanese) workplace organization method (lean manufacturing)
6 Rs	6 Rs of logistics: RIGHT quantity, object, place, time, quality and cost
7 Ps	Marketing Mix: 4 Ps + Physical Evidence, Process and People

Preface

When reading a management book that contains compelling concepts or ideas, it is a good approach to consider criticisms and drawbacks. Often, the main criticism is that the methods, ideas, concepts and models presented are too simplistic (e.g., think of SWOT-analysis, 4 Ps or 6 Rs).

What you think success looks like   **What success actually looks like**

Figure: Success according to Freeman 2019

And we can assume that this is absolutely true – for good reasons. To be clear: management is not a mathematical science (we exclude

Six Sigma at this point). In physics or electrical engineering, for example, one can model simple linear, time-invariant, causal physical systems by linear differential equations or apply the Laplace transformation (Föllinger 1990), which describe reality sufficiently enough in these particular cases. If necessary, one can always adjust the granularity or order of the models (e.g., PEST becomes PESTEL or 4 Ps become 7 Ps in marketing) (Jobber 2001).

However, management is rather different compared to science and technology, because we humans often act quite irrationally, at least we do not always behave in a causal, linear or time-invariant way. Against this background, management approaches and their limitations need to be considered critically. Management guru Henry Mintzberg rightly emphasizes that there is no universal best organization or strategy (Mintzberg et al. 1998). From this we can deduce that indeed different approaches can lead us to success if we are aware of their limitations. Furthermore, we can learn from concepts and ideas (Ritter 2022). And we need to learn (i.e., **lifelong learning**), as Peter F. Drucker calls for (Drucker 2014a).

It's a similar story with leadership. There is not one true style. Our style should always be and appear authentic. However, as long as we act in accordance with law and order, we could do virtually anything. But we must always be able to live with the consequences of our actions. This is how we should also look at the success factors and ideas in this book. They must suit us (see later also **strategic fit** according to Grant 2002 and Glossary). In any case, we must be prepared to work carefully on the implementation of our ideas, to learn and to draw the right consequences and conclusions.

When we talk about success, we have to keep in mind that there are different types of success: personal success, leadership success, career success, success as an entrepreneur and success as a company, strategic success, and so on. In this book, we will discuss a number of these types of success, focusing on the areas of business and management. However, we will not go into depth. In the following, we will refer to the original sources and our business novel (Ritter 2022). Our claim here is to list the essential aspects in the sense of a collection of formulas and to cite a few powerful quotes. The concepts and ideas presented here are primarily intended to serve as suggestions. We must find out for ourselves which of them are suitable for us personally – including our organizations – and where they can be usefully applied, and where their possible limits lie. This is not a new insight, see "Book of Five Rings" (Musashi 2021) and chapter "Strategic Success in War and Business", and it always remains our responsibility. Furthermore:

"(1) Do not feel disgusted, do not lose heart, and do not despair if you do not always succeed in realizing all your right intentions; rather, after failures, return to your resolutions and be satisfied if the majority of your actions are reasonably humane, and love what you have returned to; ..." (Marcus Aurelius in his Self-Reflections – Fifth Book, 9 (1), freely translated).

In this book we present and follow some concepts and ideas that we have developed over the last years. We will refer to them and use them as a guide and as a structure for the content of this book:

- **Criteria for successful strategies:** our basic success factors for strategies as derived from our personal experience and the works of Clausewitz, Grant, and Sunzi (Clausewitz 2003, Grant 2002, Machiavelli 2001, Sunzi 2001, Ritter 2013, 2020 and 2021).
- **Basic strategy concept:** our strategy concept based on ideas such as lean management, innovation management, entrepreneurship, Process and Design School (Drucker 2014a, Grant

2002, Hamel and Prahalad 1997, Mintzberg et al. 1998, Porter 1999, The Lean Enterprise Institute 2003, Ritter 2013 and 2020).

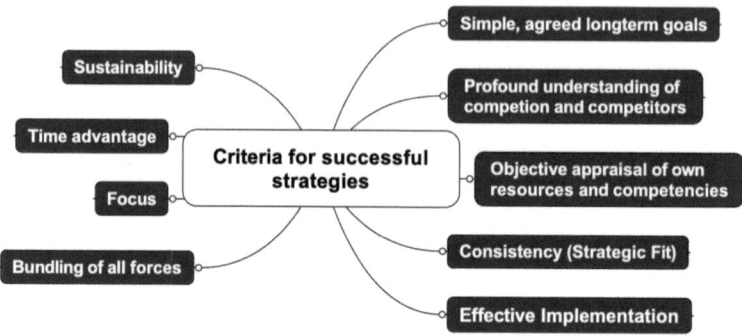

Figure: Criteria for successful strategies (as success factors) according to Ritter (2013)

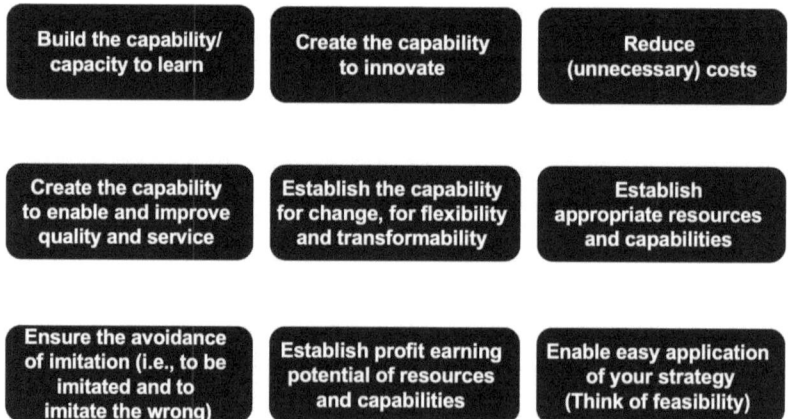

Figure: Basic strategy concept (for business success) according to Ritter (2013 and 2020)

You will notice that some publications and translations differ a bit from each other. So, when we refer to a German translation or a German source, we decided to translate (or retranslate) it into English. Our intention is to convey the basic ideas, see also **References** chapter. And as we said, you should find some concepts and ideas in this book that you can benefit from or that interest you; some also might be too complicated or not suitable for you at all. However, you should at least be aware of them. So be careful about evaluating these solutions and particularly when it comes to measuring success.

"When it's all said and done, what do we measure ourselves by? If Lansky taught me one thing, it's that there's only one measure in this world that really matters: We measure ourselves by the eyes of those we love" (Sam Worthington aka David Stone on gangster Meyer Lansky, the so-called "Mob's Accountant" played by Harvey Keitel in the 2021 film "Lansky" by Eytan Rockaway, freely translated).

Analysis

"(1) First, not arbitrarily and not without purpose. (2) Secondly, direct your striving to nothing but the goal of the common good" (Marcus Aurelius in his Self-Reflections – Twelfth Book, 20, freely translated).

When you start an academic paper or a technical project, you usually start with an analysis of the current state of the art. We decided to do our analysis according to our strategic success factors to better cluster the content, do some interviews, but also take a quick look at Wikipedia. The main criticism of Wikipedia, as we know, is that it is not really an academic or scientific source. Nonetheless, it is at least a good starting point. So, let's start with some basic insights and definitions.

Hint: If you are in a hurry, you can skip this **Analysis** chapter as we will discuss our findings and the main concepts in the following chapters. The key sources are listed in the **References** below. Furthermore, some more complementary explanations are giving in the **Glossary** below.

Success (Definition)	"Success is the state or condition of meeting a defined range of expectations. It may be viewed as the opposite of failure."
Criteria of Success	"The criteria for success depend on context, and may be relative to a particular observer or belief system. One person might consider a success what another person considers a failure, particularly in cases of direct competition or a zero-sum game. Similarly, the degree of success or failure in a situation may be differently viewed by distinct observers or participants, such that a situation that one considers to be a success, another might consider to be a failure, a qualified success or a neutral situation. For example, a film that is a commercial failure or even a box-office bomb can go on to receive a cult following, with the initial lack of commercial success even lending a cachet of subcultural coolness."
Comment	"It may also be difficult or impossible to ascertain whether a situation meets criteria for success or failure due to ambiguous or ill-defined definition of those criteria. Finding useful and effective

	criteria, or heuristics, to judge the failure or success of a situation may itself be a significant task."
The Iceberg of success	"The Iceberg of success is a specific structured model used to explain the unseen workings of an achievement. It compares what people see on the surface, to the inner complicated workings underneath the surface. Success requires hard work and dedication, most of which, people do not see and rather only see the final accomplished product. There can be great costs to success: failure, rejection, sacrifice, disappointment, hard work, dedication etc. However, once achieved, the benefits outweigh the hardships. Whilst it may be easy to assume people are lucky and achieve something by chance, often it is the hidden layers underneath the surface of the iceberg that cause this success. Whilst luck may be a factor, it is certainly not the defining characteristic of someone's ability to thrive."
In American culture	"DeVitis and Rich link the success to the notion of the American Dream. They observe that '[t]he ideal of success is found in the American Dream which is probably the most potent ideology in American life' and suggest that 'Americans generally believe in achievement, success, and materialism'. Weiss, in his study of success in the American psyche, compares the American view of success with Max Weber's concept of the Protestant work ethic."
In Biology	"Natural selection is the variation in successful survival and reproduction of individuals due to differences in phenotype. It is a key mechanism of evolution, the change in the heritable traits characteristic of a population over generations. Charles Darwin popularised the term 'natural selection', contrasting it with artificial selection, which in his view is intentional, whereas natural selection is not. As Darwin phrased it in 1859, natural selection is the 'principle by which each slight variation [of a trait], if useful, is preserved'. The concept was simple but powerful: individuals best adapted to their environments are more likely to survive and reproduce. As long as there is some variation between them and that variation is heritable, there will be an inevitable selection of individuals with the most advantageous variations. If the variations are heritable, then differential reproductive success leads to a progressive evolution of particular populations of a species, and populations that evolve to be sufficiently different eventually become different species."
In Education	"A student's success within an educational system is often expressed by way of grading. Grades may be given as numbers, letters or other symbols. By the year 1884, Mount Holyoke College was evaluating students' performance on a 100-point or percentage scale and then summarizing those numerical grades by assigning letter grades to numerical ranges. Mount Holyoke assigned letter grades A through E, with E indicating lower than

	75% performance. The A–E system spread to Harvard University by 1890. In 1898, Mount Holyoke adjusted the grading system, adding an F grade for failing (and adjusting the ranges corresponding to the other letters). The practice of letter grades spread more broadly in the first decades of the 20th century. By the 1930s, the letter E was dropped from the system, for unclear reasons. Educational systems themselves can be evaluated on how successfully they impart knowledge and skills. For example, the Programme for International Student Assessment (PISA) is a worldwide study by the Organisation for Economic Co-operation and Development (OECD) intended to evaluate educational systems by measuring 15-year-old school pupils' scholastic performance on mathematics, science, and reading. It was first performed in 2000 and then repeated every three years."
In Entrepreneur-ship	"Malcolm Gladwell's 2008 book Outliers: The Story of Success suggests that the notion of the self-made man is a myth. Gladwell argues that the success of entrepreneurs including Bill Gates is due to their circumstances, as opposed to their inborn talent."
In Philosophy of Science	"Scientific theories are often deemed successful when they make predictions that are confirmed by experiment. For example, calculations regarding the Big Bang predicted the cosmic microwave background and the relative abundances of chemical elements in deep space (see Big Bang nucleo-synthesis), and observations have borne out these predictions. Scientific theories can also achieve success more indirectly, by suggesting other ideas that turn out correct. For example, Johannes Kepler conceived a model of the solar system based on the Platonic solids. Although this idea was itself incorrect, it motivated him to pursue the work that led to the discoveries now known as Kepler's laws, which were pivotal in the development of astronomy and physics."
In Probability	"The fields of probability and statistics often study situations where events are labeled as 'successes' or 'failures'. For example, a Bernoulli trial is a random experiment with exactly two possible outcomes, 'success' and 'failure', in which the probability of success is the same every time the experiment is conducted. The concept is named after Jacob Bernoulli, a 17th-century Swiss mathematician, who analyzed them in his Ars Conjectandi (1713). The term 'success' in this sense consists in the result meeting specified conditions, not in any moral judgement. For example, the experiment could be the act of rolling a single die, with the result of rolling a six being declared a 'success' and all other outcomes grouped together under the designation 'failure'. Assuming a fair die, the probability of success would then be 1/6."

Table: Success according to Wikipedia – https://en.wikipedia.org/wiki/Success_ (concept) (Status: August 2024)

We **conducted a non-representative study** based on interviews with some high potentials (e.g., sports champions, winners of competitions in music or research, high performing students and managers). It is not representative to some extent due to the number of interviews and the very individual answers. However, the answers given were discussed with us in a very open atmosphere. Therefore, you can assume that the answers reflect the views of the interviewees relatively well. At the very least, the success factors mentioned are really relevant to them. Some individual success factors were mentioned particularly frequently, such as …

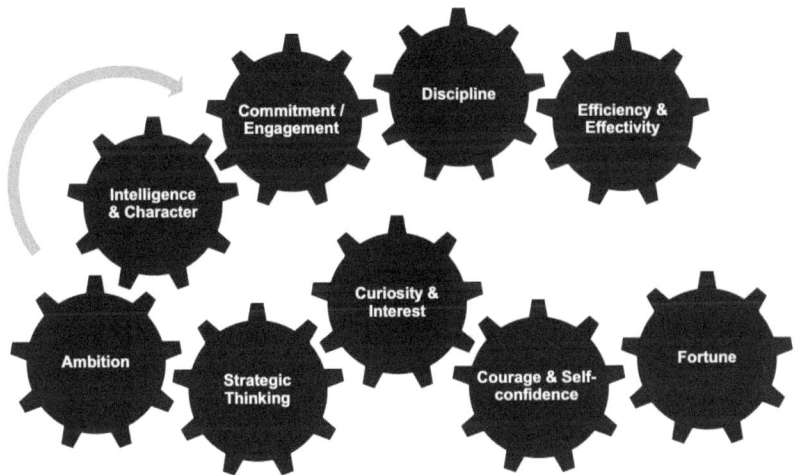

Figure: Individual success factors

We will return to some of the ideas later, see below. However, we have used this list of individual success factors to match them with our academic literature review, see next table. We will come back to the details later (see also next chapters and Glossary or References).

	Individual success factors	
		• **Collins:** "Level 5 leadership" • **Dethmer et al.:** "The 15 Commitments of Conscious Leadership" • **Drucker and Hendricks:** Focus on own strengths and exploitation of opportunities • **Frankl:** "Man's Search for Meaning" • **Machiavelli:** Ideology of "virtù" • **Marcus Aurelius:** "Self-Reflections" • **Möbius and Bigge:** The example of Helmuth von Moltke • **Nagler:** The example of Abraham Lincoln • **Schur and Weick:** Creativity, mental flexibility, sense of priorities, decisiveness, readiness for conflict and above all courage • **Senger:** Sensor for lists and kairos
A	**Intelligence & Character**	
B	**Ambition**	• **Clausewitz:** "With all your strength" • **Collins:** "Big Hairy Audacious Goals" (BHAG) • **Hamel and Prahalad:** "Strategic stretch" • **Lindenberg:** "Never doubted it" (Album/song) • See also **Lincoln, Machiavelli, Moltke, Musashi and Sunzi**
C	**Commitment / Engagement**	• **Clausewitz:** "With all your strength" • **Collins:** "Big Hairy Audacious Goals" (BHAG) • **Covey:** "7 Habits – Be Proactive" • **Hamel and Prahalad:** "Strategic stretch"
D	**Discipline**	• **Clausewitz:** Focus • **Collins:** "Culture of discipline" • **Nagler:** Never give up (see Abraham Lincoln) • See also **Musashi and Sunzi**
E	**Efficiency & Effectiveness**	• **Allan:** "Getting Things Done" • **Covey:** "7 Habits – Be Proactive, Begin with the End in Mind, Put First Things First, Think Win/Win, Seek First to Understand, Then to Be Understood, Synergize, Sharpen the Saw" • **Drucker:** "The Effective Executive" and the "seven virtues of effective leaders" • **Mackenzie:** "The Time Trap" • **Möbius and Bigge:** the example of Moltke • **Nagler:** Lincoln's "ability to pursue and name goals and visions illusionlessly and pragmatically, and to convey them in language that is as apt and clear as it is impressive" and Lincoln's "sure sense of the kairos, relevance and assertiveness of substantive concerns at a given moment"

		Individual success factors
		• **Nagler:** Lincoln's "high competence in conflict management" as well as Lincoln's striving "never … to leave anything to chance if he could influence it for himself"
F	**Strategic thinking**	• **Collins:** "Hedgehog concept" • **Covey:** "7 Habits – Begin with the End in Mind, Put First Things First, Think Win/Win" • **Drucker and Hendricks:** Focus on own strengths and opportunity exploitation • **Grant and Mintzberg:** Design and Process School • **Hendricks:** "Zone of Excellence" and "Zone of Genius" • **Khalsa:** "Helping clients succeed" • **Nagler:** Lincoln's ability to "pursue goals and visions illusionlessly and pragmatically" • See also **Clausewitz, Machiavelli, Moltke and Sunzi**
G	**Curiosity & Interest**	• **Collins, Drucker, Grant, Hamel, Prahalad and Warnecke:** Innovation as a driver • **De Geus:** Learning as a competitive factor • **Pink:** "Six Senses"
H	**Courage & Self-confidence**	• **Collins:** "Stockdale paradox" • **Hendricks:** Mastering the "Upper Limit Problem" • **Lindenberg:** "Never doubted it" (Album/song) • **Möbius and Bigge:** the example of Moltke, e.g., imperturbable calm; to "achieve a great purpose, you have to dare to do something" • **Nagler:** Lincoln's "strong willpower and ability to cope with and overcome blows of fate unbroken"
I	**Fortune**	• **Frankl:** "Der Mensch vor der Frage nach dem Sinn" and "Man's Search for Meaning" • **Hendricks:** "Zone of Genius" • **Machiavelli:** "Il Principe" ("Prince") • **Pink:** "Six Senses"

Table: Individual success factors – Consistency and overlap of the different concepts, see also page 19 and next chapters

In addition, we have used our basic strategy concept to match them with our academic literature review, see next table. We will come back to the details later (see next chapters).

	Criterion	Comment (Author: Subject/Term)
1	Establish the capability for change, for flexibility and transformability	• **Darwin:** "Survival of the fittest"; "Gradualism" • **Harari:** "Cognitive", "agricultural" and "scientific revolution" • **Machiavelli:** The lessons of the "Prince" • **Musashi:** Application and (unexpected) alternation of weapons (i.e., methods and tools)
2	Build the capability/capacity to learn	• **De Geus:** "The ability to learn faster than your competitors" • **Machiavelli, Hamel and Prahalad:** The ability to learn (including the ability to unlearn obsolete or obstructive things)
3	Create the capability to innovate	• **Drucker:** "The seven sources of innovation opportunity" • **Grant:** Product, process and strategic innovation • **Hamel:** "Future is something you create, not something that happens to you"; see also "Business Concept Innovation" • **Warnecke:** "Innovation creates future"
4	Reduce (unnecessary) costs	• Agile Management, Continuous Improvement, Gradualism, Financial Management, Zero-defects production, Lean Management and Toyota Production System (see also Neale and McElroy 2004, Ritter 2020 and 2021, The Lean Enterprise Institute 2003, Westkämper 1997) • **Porter:** "Low-cost strategy"
5	Create the capability to enable and improve quality and service	• Agile Management, Continuous Improvement, Gradualism, Financial Management, Lean Management and Toyota Production System (see also Neale and McElroy 2004, Ritter 2020 and 2021, The Lean Enterprise Institute 2003) • **Khalsa:** "Helping clients succeed" and "ORDER-Principle" • **Porter:** "Differentiation strategy"
6	Establish appropriate resources and capabilities	• **Collins:** "Hedgehog concept" • **Grant:** "Resource-based strategies" • **Khalsa:** "ORDER-Principle" • **Porter:** "Differentiation strategy"
7	Establish profit earning potential of resources and capabilities	• **Arnold:** "Value-Action Pentagon Model" • **Collins:** "Hedgehog concept"; "What drives your economic engine?" • **Grant:** "Establish profit earning potential of resources and capabilities" • **Hendricks:** "Zone of Competence", "Zone of Excellence" and "Zone of Genius"

	Criterion	Comment (Author: Subject/Term)
8	**Ensure the avoidance of imitation (i.e., to be imitated and to imitate the wrong)**	• **Grant:** "Imitation avoidance strategies": "hidden superior performance, acquisition of resources, and acquisition of capabilities and competencies that are immobile or difficult to replace (copy); competitive advantage based on multiple, distributed sources; and deterrence and retaliation" • **Senger:** Development of a sensor for stratagems
9	**Enable easy application of your strategy** **(Think of feasibility)**	• **Allen:** "Getting Things Done – Two-minute rule" • **Covey, Collins and Drucker:** Effectiveness • **(Einstein) / Scroggins:** "You have to make things as simple as possible. But not simpler" • **Grant:** "Effective implementation" • **Kalashnikov:** "Everything complicated is unnecessary, everything necessary is simple – just like my automatic rifle" • **Küstenmacher and Seiwert:** "Simplify your life" • **Möbius and Bigge:** Moltke's "inclination for simplicity" and focus on feasibility; consideration for the personality of the sub-leaders; clear commands and directives; independence of sub-leaders, decisiveness • **Other:** See also Eisenhower-Matrix or Hendricks' approach to limit oneself to only one main rule (e.g., to solve the "Upper Limit Problem") or to focus on "only" seven habits (Covey)

Table: Consistency and overlap of the different factors of the basic strategy concept (according to Ritter 2013 and 2020), see also page 14 and next chapters

Furthermore, we have used our list of strategic success factors to match them with our academic literature review, see next table. We will come back to the details later (see next chapters).

	Criterion	Comment (Author: Subject/Term)
1	Focus	• **Clausewitz** (Moltke and Sunzi): **Focus** • Collins: "Confront the brutal facts" • **Collins: "Hedgehog concept (the three circles)"** • Covey: "Be Proactive" • **Covey: "Begin with the End in Mind"** • **Covey: "Put First Things First"** • Khalsa: "Helping clients succeed" • **Hendricks: "Zone of Genius"**
2	Time advantage	• **Clausewitz, Moltke and Sunzi: Time advantage, acceleration, the right time, maturity and speed** • Collins: "First who, then what" • Covey: "Be Proactive" • Hendricks: "Einstein Time"
3	Bundling / concentration of all forces	• **Clausewitz** (Moltke and Sunzi): **Bundling / concentration of all forces** • Collins: "Confront the brutal facts" • Collins: "Hedgehog concept (the three circles)" • Collins: "Technology accelerators" • **Collins: "No tyranny of the OR – embrace the genius of the AND"** • **Hamel and Prahalad: "Strategic stretch"** and **"Resource leverage"**
4	Sustainability	• **Clausewitz** (Moltke and Sunzi): **Sustainability** • **Collins: "First who, then what"; "flywheel"; "Hedgehog concept (the three circles)"; "culture of discipline"; "preserving the core" / "fostering evolution"** • **Covey: "Think Win/Win"; "Seek First to Understand, Then to Be Understood"; "Synergize"; "Sharpen the Saw"** • **Hamel: "Business Concept Innovation"** • **Hendricks: "Zone of Genius"** • **Khalsa: "Helping clients succeed"** • **Machiavelli: Transformability** • **Ritter: "Basic Strategy Concept"**
5	Simple, agreed long-term goals	• **Collins:** "Level 5 leadership" (skills); "First who, then what"; "Confront the brutal facts; **"Hedge-hog concept (the three circles)"**; "More than profits – find your organization's purpose and **build the core ideology"** • **Covey: "Begin with the End in Mind"** • **Grant: "Simple, agreed long-term goals"** • **Hendricks: "Zone of Genius"**

	Criterion	Comment (Author: Subject/Term)
		• **Khalsa: "Helping clients succeed"** • **Möbius and Bigge: the example of Moltke; Think of feasibility**
6	**Profound understanding of competition and competitors**	• Collins: "Hedgehog concept (the three circles)" • **Grant** (Moltke and Sunzi)**: "Profound understanding of competition and competitors"** • Khalsa: "Helping clients succeed"
7	**Objective appraisal of own resources and competencies**	• **Collins:** "Level 5 leadership" (skills); "Confront the brutal facts"; **"Hedgehog concept (the three circles)"**; "Technology accelerators" • **Grant** (Moltke and Sunzi)**: Objective appraisal of own resources and competencies** • **Hendricks: "Zone of Genius"** • Khalsa: "Helping clients succeed" • Möbius and Bigge: the example of Moltke. Think of feasibility
8	**Consistency (Strategic Fit)**	• **Collins: "Hedgehog concept (the three circles)"; "Culture of discipline";** "Preserve the core / stimulate progress – change everything readily, except the core beliefs and values" • **Grant: "Strategic Fit"** • Hamel: "Business Concept Innovation" • **Hendricks: "Zone of Genius"** • Khalsa: "Helping clients succeed" • **Möbius and Bigge:** Moltke's focus on feasibility
9	**Effective implementation**	• **Balogun and Hope Hailey: "Change Kaleidoscope"** • **Collins: "Level 5 leadership" (skills); "First who, then what";** "Hedgehog concept (the three circles)"**; "Culture of discipline"; "Technology accelerators";** "Clock building, not time telling – go beyond a great leader and building a great institution; preserve the core / stimulate progress – change everything readily, except the core beliefs and values" • **Covey:** "Be Proactive"; "Begin with the End in Mind"; **"Put First Things First";** "Think Win/Win"; "Seek First to Understand, Then to Be Understood"; "Synergize"; **"Sharpen the Saw"** • **Dethmer et al.: "15 Commitments of conscious leadership"** • **Grant: Effective implementation** • **Hamel: "Business Concept Innovation"** • Khalsa: "Helping clients succeed"

Criterion	Comment (Author: Subject/Term)
	• **Hendricks: "Zone of Genius";** master the **"Upper Limit Problem"** • **Möbius and Bigge: The example of Moltke — to educate subordinate to act independently and focus on feasibility** • Ritter: Think like a "control loop"

Table: Consistency and overlap of success factors. **Bold:** high degree of agreement with criterion, see also page 14 and next chapters

Two remarks: First, our selection is not all-inclusive and remains quite selective. Second, the assignment of our criteria to concepts and references shows that we are on the trail of the core ideas.

"These three things, to recognize oneself, to avoid evil company, and to remain steadfast, this pious man undoubtedly considered good and necessary because he practiced them himself, and that he did not fail in doing so; for having recognized himself, he has not only fled evil societies, but also the whole world, and has persevered in such a resolution to the end, on which without a doubt blessedness hangs, but in what way follows hereafter," is how Simplicissimus summarizes the last words addressed to him by his father, the hermit, in the "Abenteuerlichen Simplicissimus Teutsch" (1668), freely translated, before the latter lays himself to die in the grave previously dug by both of them. The hermit was an extremely pragmatic man. Covey would say: "Begin with the End in Mind" (see page 41).

Success Through Evolution

"(1) That shortly you will be no one and nowhere, and that also nothing of what you now see and no one of those who now live will be. (2) Because everything is created by nature to transform, to change and to perish, so that afterwards something else can come into being" (Marcus Aurelius in his Self-Reflections – Twelfth Book, 21, freely translated).

"It is not the most intellectual of the species that survives; it is not the strongest that survives; but the species that survives is the one that is able best to adapt and adjust to the changing environment in which it finds itself" (This is how Leon C. Megginson summarizes the ideas of Charles Robert Darwin, 1964); https://quoteinvestigator. com/2014/05/04/adapt/ (Status: August 2024)).

From the wealth of books on the history of mankind and science, we would like to recommend three books: Bill Bryson's "A short History of Almost Everything", Simonyi's "Kulturgeschichte der Physik" and Yuval Noah Harari's "A Brief History of humankind" (Bryson 2005, Harari 2015, Simonyi 1995). Many lessons can be learned from these, e.g., Charles Darwin's theory of evolution or the three revolutions according to Harari: the "cognitive revolution", the "agricultural revolution" and the "scientific revolution". But, to make a long story short; for us, there are three universal success factors that have played an important role during human evolution (see also Ritter 2022):

1) **transformability** (being able to change and adapt),
2) **ability for cooperation** (communication and organization) and
3) **inspiration** (developing a vision including leadership).

In the following chapters, we will also discuss the importance of communication, transformability and leadership in more detail.

"**The ability to learn faster than your competitors** may be your only sustainable competitive advantage" (De Geus 1988).

"Adapt yourself to the things with which your lot has brought you together. And the people with whom fate has brought you together, love them, but sincerely" (Marcus Aurelius in his Self-Reflections – Sixth Book, 39, freely translated).

"For if a man behaves with prudence and patience, and the circumstances of the time are such that his course of action is good, he succeeds in his undertaking; but if the circumstances change, he perishes, because he does not change his course of action. Now man is seldom so wise as to be able to adapt himself to this change, partly because he cannot leave the path which his natural disposition points out to him, partly because one who has always been fortunate in a chosen path cannot convince himself that it would be good to leave it" (Machiavelli in "Il Principe" (i.e., "The Prince"), written in 1513, freely translated).

Ad 1: Transformability (Adaptability, changeability, mutability or flexibility) are seen as fundamental success factor (see Darwin's theory of evolution or Machiavelli's advice in "Il Principe", i.e., the "Prince"). It is important to understand that transformability (see Westkämper 1999) includes **learning and forgetting** (see Machiavelli's quote or Hamel and Prahalad 1997, see also page 89) and the **ability to implement change effectively and efficiently** (see Balogun and Hope Hailey's Change Kaleidoscope, see also pages 105-109).

Ad 2: Ability for cooperation (i.e., appropriate organization, communication, management and implementation); with all of your decisions, one can of course make crucial mistakes. Our task and responsibility are to avoid as many errors as possible (see also pages 100-119). Therefore, we would like to emphasize once again that adequate communication (see Mackenzie 1997 and Drucker 2014, see also pages 36 and 66) in change processes or strategic initiatives contributes significantly to success. The **ability to organize, communicate and cooperate** with each other efficiently or effectively we also consider as another major success factor (see Drucker 2014a and 2014b, Harari 2015, Nagler 2015, Möbius and Bigge 2023).

"If you want to build a ship, don't gather the men to find the wood, prepare the tools or divide up the work and delegate tasks – instead teach the men the longing for the endless, wide ocean" (according to Antoine de Saint-Exupéry; the original source of this quote is not clear).

Ad 3: The power of myths and the ability to inspire others (see Harari 2015 and 2019 and the "Cultural Web") is an additional important success factor. The **Cultural Web** is a framework, which goes back to Johnson and Scholes, enables the analysis and design of organizations in the context of "change" according to the (technical) dimension (organizational structures, control system), its political dimension (formal and informal power structures) and its cultural manifestation (routines, rituals, "stories" and symbols). Balogun and Hope Hailey consider the Cultural Web as an essential lever for change.

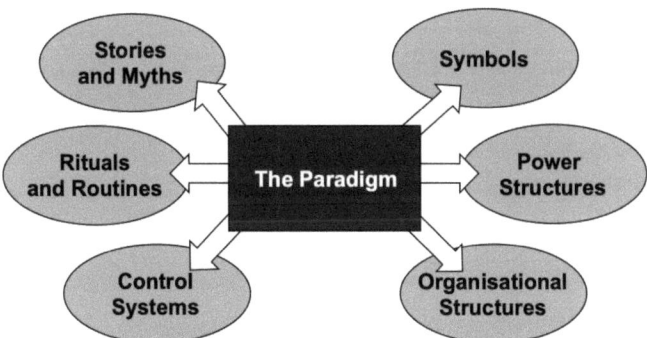

Figure: Cultural Web according to Johnson & Scholes (Balogun and Hope Hailey 2004)

Transformability (Westkämper 1999), **good communication** (Drucker 2014b), **good cooperation skills and shared values and visions** are not only essential for organizations to survive. These skills also represent **important success factors for us as individuals**.

"He who stops getting better has stopped being good" (probably quote from John Andrewes in 1615), see also "Qui cessat esse melior, cessat esse bonus" or "Hee that ceasseth to be better, ceasseth to be good" (https://quoteinvestigator.com/2019/10/27/good-better/ (Status: August 2024)). Hint: see also TQM and kaizen (Glossary).

"If something is difficult for you to accomplish, do not believe that it is impossible for man in itself, but if something is possible and appropriate for man, believe that this is attainable for you as well" (Marcus Aurelius in his Self-Reflections – Sixth Book, 19, freely translated).

We have already mentioned some individual success factors such as **intelligence** and **character, ambition, commitment** (including engagement), **discipline, efficiency** and **effectiveness, strategic thinking, curiosity** and **interest, courage and self-confidence,** and **fortune** in the analysis chapter. In addition, we emphasize that the strategic success factors such as **focus, concentration of all forces** are also essential for success (see Clausewitz 2003 and page 99). There is another factor that our father/grandfather pointed out and that we call the **Papa-Rolf-Benno principle**.

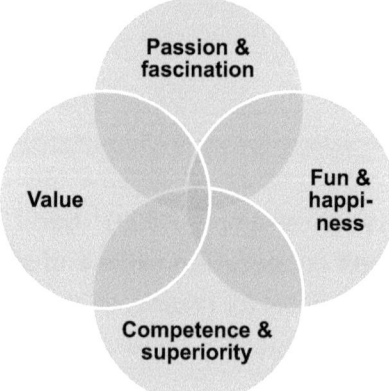

Figure: Papa-Rolf-Benno principle for success (see also page 115)

"Guys, choose a profession or a course of study **that really interests** and excites you, that is, something that **matches your inclinations**. Then you will automatically be better than the average. Always strive to **be better** than your competitors. And when choosing your course of study, **make sure that it is not a useless art** … Finally: become happy and **enjoy what you are doing**" (Papa-Rolf-Benno principle).

You will find out that it is align with the Collins' Hedgehog concept. In this chapter, we would like to focus on three general aspects of personal success: 1) our **ability to prevent or enable success** which Gay Hendricks call our "Upper Limit Problem", 2) **efficiency** and 3) **effectiveness**. Our responsibility is to avoid as many mistakes as possible. Let's start with this: **Eliminate obstacles**.

"NO PANIC," see "The Hitchhiker's Guide to the Galaxy" (Adams 2000).

"Never take counsel of your fears" (General Thomas Jonathan Jackson, nicknamed "Stonewall Jackson", see https://beruhmte-zitate.de/zitate/131170-andrew-jackson-angst-ist-ein-schlechter-ratgeber/ (Status: August 2024)).

Ad 1: Fear should never guide us in a negative sense (fear should only keep us from doing stupid or bad things). This is a universal rule – for every area of life. Also, we are not victims. That sounds a lot like Viktor Frankl, a survivor of the Holocaust (Frankl 2019 and 2020).

And we are **responsible** for our own success. That's why Hendricks challenges us to **overcome our barriers**. In this context, he distinguishes four areas of competence:

1 THE ZONE OF INCOMPETENCE	**4 THE ZONE OF GENIUS**
2 THE ZONE OF COMPETENCE	**3 THE ZONE OF EXCELLENCE**

Table: "4 main zones of activities" according to Hendricks (2009)

"(3) Don't you realize how much you already have to offer that you can't plead lack of talent and inability? And yet you still remain of your own free will on your low level?" (Marcus Aurelius in his Self-Reflections – Fifth Book, 5 (3), freely translated).

One of the secrets of Moltke's success was **to focus on what was feasible** (Möbius and Bigge 2023). In the "Effective Executive" (Drucker 2014b), Peter Drucker urged us to **focus on our own strengths** (the strengths of our superiors, colleagues, and subordinates; and on the "strengths" of the situation, i.e., what we can do). We should **never focus** (only) **on weaknesses** (i.e., our "Zone of incompetence") or on **things we cannot manage**. Similarly, Hendricks urges us to focus primarily on our area of excellence or on our **area of genius**. You can find the details in the remarkable book "The Big Leap" (Hendricks 2009) and some extracts in the next table.

	THE BIG LEAP – Conquer Your Hidden Fear and Take Life to the Next Level	
1	Remove Your Last Obstacle to Ultimate Success in Wealth, Work, and Love	**The one problem that holds you back & the moment of discovery** • **The Upper Limit Problem is our universal human tendency to sabotage ourselves.** • **The Upper Limit Problem is caused by a too-low thermostat setting on our ability to achieve and enjoy our ultimate success.**
2	Preparing for your Big Leap	**The One Problem and How to Solve it** • **THE UPPER LIMIT PROBLEM: preventing us to reach Zone of Genius** • Consequence: **staying in the Zone of Incompetence, Competence or Excellence**, instead of reaching the Zone of Genius
3	Making the Big Leap	**Dismantling the Foundation of the Problem** • Hidden Barrier no. 1: Feeling Fundamentally Flawed • Hidden Barrier no. 2: Disloyalty and Abandonment • Hidden Barrier no. 3: Believing That More Success Brings a Bigger Burden • Hidden Barrier no. 4: The Crime of Outshining
4	Getting Specific	**How to Spot the Upper Limit Problem in Daily Life** • Typical ways we upper-limit ourselves: worry, criticism and blame, deflecting, squabbling, getting sick or getting hurt

		THE BIG LEAP – Conquer Your Hidden Fear and Take Life to the Next Level
		• Upper limit behaviors: hiding significant feelings, not keeping agreements, not speaking significant truths to the relevant people • The Three Ps: punishment, prevention and protection
5	**Building a New Home in Your Zone of Genius**	**How to Make Every Moment an Expression of Your Genius** • The Genius Question no. 1: **What do I most love to do?** (I love so much I can do it for long stretches of time without getting tired or bored.) • The Genius Question no. 2: **What work do I do that doesn't seem like work?** (I can do it all day long without ever feeling tired or bored.) • The Genius Question no. 3: **In my work, what produces the highest ratio of abundance and satisfaction to amount of time spent?** (Even if I do only ten seconds or a few minutes of it, an idea or a deeper connection may spring forth that leads to huge value.) • The genius Question no. 4: **What is my unique ability?** (There's a special skill I'm gifted with. This unique ability, fully realized and put to work, can provide enormous benefits to me and any organization I serve.)
6	**Living in Your Zone of Genius**	**Using the Ultimate Success Mantra to Thrive in Love, Abundance, and Creativity** • Out of the box and onto the spiral • The ultimate success mantra: a central guiding intention • The enlighted NO – turn down something that doesn't fit in your Zone of Genius • Renewing and refining commitment
7	**Living in Einstein Time**	**Creating Time for Full Expression of Your Genius** When we switch to Einstein Time, we take charge of the amount of time we have. We realize that we're where time comes from. We embrace this liberating insight: since I'm the producer of time, I can make as much of it as I need. • Where in my life am I not taking full ownership? • What am I trying to disown? • What aspects of my life do I need to take full ownership of?
8	**Solving the Relationship Problem**	**Transcending the Upper Limits of Love and Appreciation** • Unsatisfying relationships: devitalized, passive-congenial and conflict-habituated relationship • Plenty time for yourself, put a priority on speaking the microscopic truth …

Table: Insights from "The Big Leap" according to Hendricks (2009)

Since the **"Upper Limit Problem is our universal human tendency to sabotage ourselves"**, we must be aware of this problem in order to overcome it (manage the hidden barriers). With certainty, **we can at least push the boundaries**. Furthermore, we need to **find our "unique ability"** (remember this when we discuss the "Hedgehog concept").

> "There are no street signs in the jungle. You have to find your own way" (Udo Lindenberg in his song "Niemals dran gezweifelt" (= "Never doubted it"), freely translated).

We also **need a strong will to win in order to succeed**. Otherwise, we will fail, as Kensei Musashi has already recognized.

> "No matter how important the opponent is, you must never think he is superior. Otherwise, you have already lost the fight" (Musashi 2021, freely translated).

Ad 2: Apart from this limiting factor, we need to consider two other aspects to be successful: efficiency and effectiveness. Next, let's take a look at **efficiency ("Do things right")**. There is a vast amount of literature and methods on how we can become more efficient personally or as managers. Certainly, efficiency is important to our daily work. Therefore, let's take up some core ideas like David Allen's **"Getting Things Done"** (Allen 2001). The basic criticism of "Getting Things Done" – and to be fair, this must apply to many other methods as well – is that the method was not developed scientifically (if that bothers you at all). Furthermore, there are no empirical values available to what extent the method actually contributes to an increase in efficiency, although numerous users are absolutely convinced of it. Basically, we ourselves consider proper delegation and getting things done quickly (the so-called **two-minute rule**) to be good practice, see below.

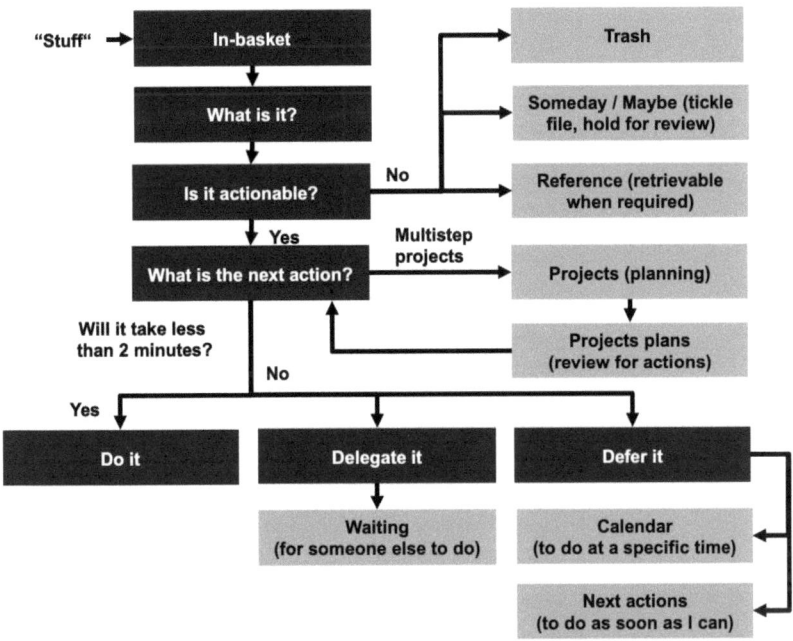

Figure: "Getting Things Done" – workflow-diagram according to David Allen (2001)

Remark: We need also free space including contingency plans for important things (see TUDAPOL principle, Ritter 2020, see also pages 110-112). If you are looking for an even simpler method, **remember the Eisenhower Matrix** (see Glossary), which of course has a few drawbacks. With the book **"The Time Trap"** (Mackenzie 1997), another important contribution to self-management is provided. Mackenzie and his team have repeatedly asked their numerous customers about the "Time Wasters" over more than two decades and have developed many ideas for solutions.

The Twenty Biggest Time Wasters		
	Time Waster	**Causes**
1	**Attempting too much**	Unaware of importance, lack of priorities and planning, unrealistic time estimates, responding to the urgent, over-response, overambition and inordinate need to achieve, desire to impress boss, overdesire to appear cooperative, understaffed, perfectionism
2	**Poor communi-cation**	Unaware of importance, lack of time, not listening / inatten-tive, purpose not clear, use of wrong channel, poor timing, insufficient communication, lack of receptivity, differing value systems, lack of feedback
3	**Confused respon-sibility or authority**	Failure to clarify precise responsibility with manager or partner, lack of position / job description, job description overlaps others, usurping of authority by others, responsi-bility without authority, nondescriptive titles, confused or no organization chart, generic job descriptions, lack of emphasis on assumption of responsibility and exercise of initiative, employees unwilling to accept responsibility
4	**Ineffective delegation**	Insecurity / fear of failure, lack confidence in staff, giving unclear, incomplete, or confused instructions, can do the job better and faster yourself, more comfortable doing than managing, expect everyone to know the details, failure to establish appropriate controls, overcontrol, failure to follow-up, understaffed / overworked sub-ordinates, no one to dele-gate to
5	**Drop-in visitors**	No plan for handling, ego, feeling of importance, desire to be available, no plans for unavailability, fear of offending, open-door policy, requiring or expecting subordinates to check with you excessively, inability to terminate visits, boss, persistent friends, poor physical location, heavy traffic pattern, exposed, without door or personal office, client's desire to be helpful
6	**Inability to say No**	Desire to win approval, acceptance, fear of offending, pos-sess capabilities in demand, false sense of obligation, not knowing how to refuse, lack excuses, no time to think of an-swer or excuse, lack objectives and priorities, thoughtless as-sumptions by others that you will say yes, can't say no to boss
7	**Incomplete information**	Unaware of importance, lack system, difficult to know what information is needed, failure to test its reliability, providing information not needed or requested, failure to assess prior-ity or urgency of requested information, failure to anticipate probable delays in obtaining information, lack of authority to require information needed, indecision or delay by others in providing needed information, support staff uninformed
8	**Leaving tasks unfinished**	Unaware of the problem, lack objectives, priorities, and dead-lines, failure to reward self, responding to the urgent, clut-tered desk / personal disorganization, lack determination to

The Twenty Biggest Time Wasters		
	Time Waster	Causes
		complete tasks (lack self-discipline, lazy), inability to delegate, accepting interruptions, shifting priorities, incomplete or unreliable information blocks task completion
9	Management by crisis	Unaware of importance, failure to anticipate problems and to develop contingency plans, overreaction (treating problems as crisis), firefighting, procrastination, unrealistic time estimates, mechanical breakdown / human error, reluctance of staff to break bad news, overreaction engendered by VIP request, failure to establish controls
10	Meetings	Lack of purpose, lack of agenda, wrong people / too many / too few, no planning, too many / too few meetings, not starting / ending on time, allowing interruptions, wandering from agenda, failure to summarize conclusions, failure to follow-up
11	Paperwork	Indecision, procrastination, not delegating, perfectionism, hoarding, overfilling, leaving tasks unfinished, attempting too much at once, lack system, slow reader
12	Personal disorganization	Unaware of importance, lack system, ego (viewed by some as a symbol of business, importance, indispensability), fear loss of control, fear of forgetting, allowing interruptions, procrastination / indecision, lack objectives, priorities, and daily plan, failure to delegate, failure to screen, failure to use available tools
13	Inadequate planning	Unaware of importance, lack system, lack time to plan, crisis-oriented (assumes crisis are unavoidable), lack self-discipline, fear of commitment, lack of job description, difficulty of assigning priorities to tasks, assumptions that since few days are typical, it is futile to plan, or that emergencies will spoil plans anyway, have plan in mind but believe it is not important enough to write it down
14	Procrastination	Inability to identify, ego trip (crisis creating), thinking I work best under pressure, habit of doing the easy or trivial first, postponing the difficult, unrealistic time estimates, attempting too much, lack regular monitoring of progress, lack of self-discipline, leaving tasks unfinished, lack of deadlines, fear that the task will be too difficult, fear of boredom
15	Inadequate controls and progress reports	Unaware of importance, lack of familiarity with tools, belief that sound plans somehow achieve themselves, lack enforcement of controls and progress reports now in place
16	Lack of self-discipline	Lack objectives or standards, lack of planning and priorities, not setting deadlines, not following up, not using available tools and techniques, lack of interest, leaving tasks unfinished, daydreaming, procrastination, bad habits

The Twenty Biggest Time Wasters		
Time Waster		**Causes**
17	**Socializing**	Need to change pace occasionally and desire for change of scenery, gregarious instinct / enjoy socializing, curiosity, desire to stay informed, fear of offending, inability to terminate conversation, inability to say no, thinking it is important for your business, boss, persistent friends, poor physical location, heavy traffic patterns, exposed, without door or personal office
18	**Inadequate staff**	Unaware of importance, remaining uninvolved or not supporting training, poor selection procedures, lack of adequate needs assessment, lack follow-up, limited finances, poor time use by present staff, priority projects not handled, fear that only you can do the work
19	**Telephone interruptions**	No plan for handling, no plans for unavailability, lack of delegation, inability to terminate conversation, ineffective screening, no support staff, answer your own policy, poor telephone system, no one else available to answer phones, socializing to avoid dull tasks
20	**Travel**	Purpose unclear, not exploring alternatives, forgetting to take important things with you, poor use of time en route, poor scheduling, stacked desk upon return, changing or rescheduling trip

Table: "The Twenty Biggest Time Wasters" according to Alec MacKenzie in "The Time Trap" (1997)

It pays to deal with these time wasters in order to be successful. And don't forget: Efficiency (and effectiveness) is primarily associated with **simplification**. This insight is not really new.

"Everything complicated is unnecessary, everything necessary is simple – just like my automatic rifle"; see Reuters interview on Mikhail Kalashnikov's 90th birthday: "When a young man, I read somewhere the following: God the Almighty said, 'All that is too complex is unnecessary, and it is simple that is needed' ... So, this has been my lifetime motto – I have been creating weapons to defend the borders of my fatherland, to be simple and reliable" (Mikhail Kalashnikov), see also Solowjow (Status: August 2024).

"Everything must be made as simple as possible. But not simpler" (allegedly Albert Einstein, probably quotation of the lyricist Mark Scroggins; https://quoteinvestigator.com/2011/05/13/einstein-simple/ (Status: August 2024)).

Keep this in mind. In addition, Werner Tiki Küstenmacher and Lothar Seiwert offered some useful tips in **"Simplify your life"** in the early 2000s (Küstenmacher und Seiwert 2003) (i.e., a kind of "Lean thinking", see also Glossary – Lean Lexicon), although their critics point out that it includes rather plain and banal job and life advice. Their ideas have an empirical character (they are mainly not scientifically derived or statistically proven), but can be considered good practice. As is so often the case, one can think of such books as a wonder bag of which we can pick out the things that seem suitable for us personally.

Another factor to be successful is to **master complexity**. In industry, the concept of **Lean Management** and the **Toyota Production System (TPS)** were developed over several decades to deal with complexity in production and become sustainably successful (The Lean Enterprise Institute 2003), see also Glossary.

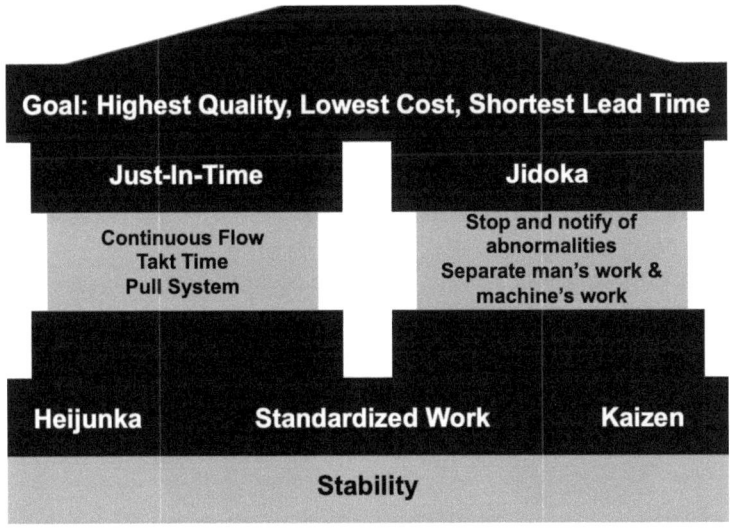

Figure: Toyota Production System "House" (The Lean Enterprise Institute 2003)

In general, the approach is based on lean management principles such as **standardization**, **elimination of waste** (the so-called seven wastes such as unnecessary rework, overproduction – remember the 20-time wasters?), **kanban**, **heijunka**, **continuous improvement** (kaizen), **just-in-time**, **takt time**, **continuous flow**, etc. (see Glossary). In the broadest sense, this also includes simplification and the reduction of complexity, such as a tidy workplace or a workplace where only the tools that are really needed are stored in the best possible position (see also the so-called "5 Ss"). And as Musashi said (see the "Book of Five Rings", Musashi 2021), "pay attention to even the smallest little things". Hint: In system and model building, we apply models that, for example, have exactly the system order that is really needed (e.g., for simulations). The reduction of complexity is therefore often an important step.

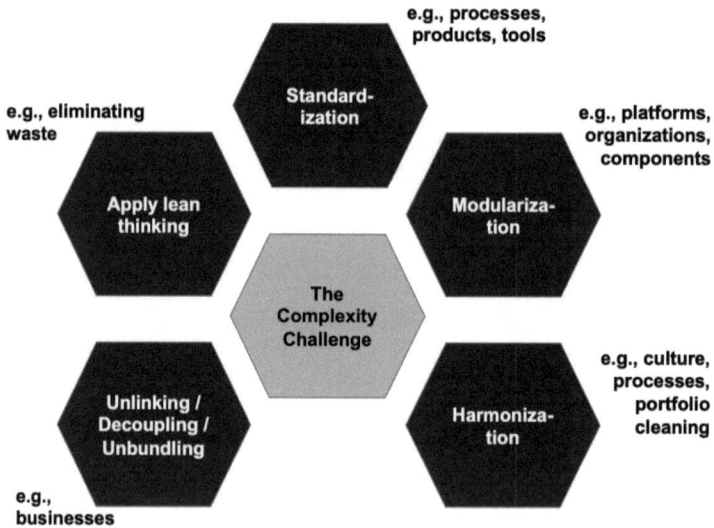

Figure: How to reduce and master complexity, see also Ritter 2020

Ad 3: Efficiency is very important. But there is another point that seems much more important to us: **effectiveness ("Do the right things")**. It is comparable to the ratio of productivity to profitability or profitability to liquidity. Profitability is important, but **profitability without liquidity is deadly**. **Efficiency without effectiveness is useless**: **Do the right things right!** We have already mentioned Gay Hendricks. Two other prominent exponents explaining effectiveness in leadership and life are Peter Drucker and Stephen Covey, see "The Effective Executive" (Drucker 2014b) and "The 7 Habits of Highly Effective People" (Covey 2020). We'll come back to Drucker when we talk about success in leadership. Of course, his ideas can also be applied to personal success (e.g., taking responsibility for our decisions).

"In my experience, **effective leaders don't start with their tasks, they start with their time** ... An effective leader knows that he can't optimize his use of time until he figures out where his time actually goes ... To be effective, every knowledge worker, and especially the leader, must **have fairly large, continuous blocks of time**. A few minutes here and there are not enough even if they add up to an impressive number of hours" (Drucker 2014b, freely translated). Comment: Furthermore, provide **additional time buffers and free spaces** (Ritter 2020).

For Covey, seven habits are essential for our personal success.

The 7 Habits of Highly Effective / Ineffective People		
Private Victory		
Habit 1	**Be Proactive**	React
Habit 2	**Begin with the End in Mind**	**Begin with the Squat in Mind**
Habit 3	**Put First Things First**	**Put First Things Last**
Public Victory – Paradigms of Interdependence		
Habit 4	**Think Win/Win**	**Think Win/Lose**
Habit 5	**Seek First to Understand, Then to Be Understood**	**Seek First to Talk, Then Pretend to Listen**
Habit 6	**Synergize**	**Be an Island**
Renewal		
Habit 7	**Sharpen the Saw**	**Burn Yourself Out**

Table: "The 7 Habits of Highly Effective People" according to Covey (2020). Comment: The right column has been added later by Covey's son, Sean.

The seven habits include proactivity, goal orientation, setting the right priorities, striving for WIN/WIN situations, understanding our counterparts, using synergies and appropriate implementation. It is quite obvious that Covey's habits, e.g., no. 4 can be quite controversial (think monopolies and "the winner takes it all"). Furthermore, Covey distinguishes four types of activities (think Eisenhower matrix: **Do the right things right** = Do the most important AND the most urgent things first! The Covey approach deviates from this): For important things it is necessary to tackle them early enough, but moreover to give them enough time and space. A very good wine needs to mature.

Time Management-Matrix		
	Urgent	**Not Urgent**
Important	I) Activities: • Crises • Pressing problems • Deadline-driven projects	II) Activities: • Prevention, production capability activities • Relationship building • Recognizing new opportunities • Planning, recreation
Not important	III) Activities: • Interruptions, some calls • Some mail, some reports • Some meetings • Proximate, pressing matters • Popular activities	IV) Activities: • Trivia, busywork • Some mail • Some phone calls • Time wasters • Pleasant activities

Table: Time management according to Covey (2020)

I Results: • Stress • Burnout • Crisis management • Always putting out fires	II
III	IV

Table: Time management results according to Covey (2020)

I		II
III Results: • Short-term focus • Crisis management • Reputation-chameleon character • See goals and plans as worthless • Feel victimized, out of control • Shallow or broken relationships		**IV**

Table: Time management results according to Covey (2020)

I III	II IV
Results: • Total irresponsibility • Fired from jobs • Dependent on others or institutions for basics	

Table: Time management results according to Covey (2020)

I	II
Results: • Vision, perspective • Balance, discipline • Control, few crises	

Table: Time management results according to Covey (2020)

Time Management-Matrix		
	Urgent	**Not Urgent**
Important	**I THE PROCRASTINATOR:** • Crises • Emergency meetings • Last-minute deadlines • Pressing problems • Unforeseen events	**II THE PRIORITIZER:** • Proactive work • High-impact goals • Creative thinking • Planning and prevention • Relationship building • Learning and renewal
Not important	**III THE YES-MAN:** • Needless interruptions • Unnecessary reports • Irrelevant meetings • Other's people minor issues; popular activities • Unimportant e-mail, tasks, phone calls, status posts, etc.	**IV THE SLACKER:** • Trivial work • Avoidance activities • Excessive relaxation, television, gaming, internet • Time wasters • Gossip

Table: "The 7 Habits of Highly Effective People" according to Covey (2020)

Time Management-Matrix				
	Urgent		**Not Urgent**	
Important	I **NECESSITY** XXX = XXX		II **EXTRAORDINARY PRODUCTIVITY** XXX = XXXXXXXX	
	Time + Energy	Return	Time + Energy	Return
Not important	III **DISTRACTION** XXXXXX = XXX		IV **WASTE** XXX = 0	
	Time + Energy	Return	Time + Energy	Return

Table: "The 7 Habits of Highly Effective People" according to Covey (2020)

As you can see, the different activities provide different positive or negative results. **Focus on the important, avoid waste!**

***

Remark: If you are looking for examples of truly effective people, you should read biographies of great men and women in science, business, politics, or the fields that affects you personally.

"Lincoln's personal qualities and experiences must undoubtedly be taken into account if his success in Chicago is to be adequately explained. He had been confronted with enough defeats in his life, which, compared to that of his rivals, had been without privileges. From each one, it seems, he **had learned never to give up or to leave something to chance if he could influence it for himself**. This explains his **intensive networking**, his extensive correspondence, his cunning tactics behind the scenes before the Convention. Unlike his opponents, he had been willing to raise his profile through extensive speaking tours. His months of business travel in Judge Davis' entourage and his previous resume had made him persistent, pugnacious, and also modest" (Professor Jörg Nagler on Abraham Lincoln's path to the White House and intra-party victory to the presidential nomination in "Abraham Lincoln – America's Great President", freely translated).

Career and Success

"(1) Never consider anything useful for you, which could force you once to break loyalty, to lose reverence, to hate someone, to harbor suspicion, to wish evil to someone, to pretend, and to desire something that should be hidden by the walls and curtains" (Marcus Aurelius in his Self-Reflections – Third Book, 7 (1) freely translated).

"Yeah, 'someday'. That's a dangerous word." – "Dangerous?" – "It's really just code for 'never'. I think a lot about things I haven't done" (Tom Cruise aka Roy Miller to Cameron Diaz aka June in "Knight and Day").

When we talk about success, we have to keep in mind that there are different types of success: personal success, leadership success, career success, success as an entrepreneur and success as a company, strategic success, and so on. Now let's look at professional success, because there are some additional peculiarities worth mentioning. It is not fundamentally wrong to assume that the success factors considered so far, e.g., for personal success and, as we will see later, for strategic success, can of course also be applied to a successful career: e.g., being efficient and effective or mastering the "Upper Limit Problem" (e.g., "Believing that more success brings a bigger burden").

When we talk about careers, we think primarily of success in an organization such as a political party, in the military, or in a company. So, we are talking about people who are in employment in the broadest sense (e.g., employed managers). This is where, for example, intrapreneurs and, above all, entrepreneurs differ to some extent. On the subject of career success, as is often the case, there is also a huge selection of literature and self-help books. At this point, we would like to remind you of "Dilbert" and the ironically sarcastic books by Scott Adams, from which, the more experienced will definitely confirm, many lessons can be learned (Adams 1998).

"How you assert yourself: ... Use sarcasm. People with bad ideas, by definition, can't be bothered by logic. If they thought logically, they wouldn't have bad ideas – unless the ideas were based on false data. This gives you two strategies to bring down an illogical idea: 1.) Argue with facts. Do extensive research to show weaknesses in the other person's argument. 2) Use sarcasm to ridicule the idea and make the person look like a fool" (Adams 1998, freely translated).

Furthermore, we refer to "Wahnsinnskarriere" (i.e., "Crazy Career"), a German business novel (Schur and Weick 2005), which provides interesting insights into the topic of opportunism and unscrupulousness in personal advancement (see also Machiavelli 2001 and 2021), although it has been quite controversial. At the very least, one can better understand why some politicians and managers were able to rise rapidly in their organizations without ever having delivered anything profitable (before disappearing from the scene again). The ideas and theses from "Wahnsinnskarriere" still originate from the "last millennium". There is no doubt that our values and, to some extent, our customs (see home office and parental leave) can and have changed somewhat. In our business novel, we had our fictional friend Quentin comment on the weaknesses and consequences of these career tips (Ritter 2022).

Tips & Tricks	Comment / Quotation
Initial conditions	• **The right company:** "There is a rule of thumb: It is first more important to be on the right train than to be in the right coach class." • **Education:** "One thing you should definitely not do as a career-oriented person: develop the ambition to hand in a particularly important or a particularly good doctoral thesis. After all, you don't want to work scientifically later on, but make a career in business." • **Age:** "If you want to make a career, you should take your time with your first job. You should study in peace and make sure that the fun in life is not neglected. This promotes composure and emotional intelligence. ... In the eyes of others, you are always too young for a job; until the time when you are much too old for it."

Table: Tips and tricks for a "Crazy career" according to Schur and Weick (2005), freely translated

Tips & Tricks	Comment / Quotation
Important techniques **Figures**	• "There is a hierarchy of numbers. By far the most unimportant are frequently changing individual values. With their short half-life and low information content, they are not suitable for long-term memorization or recommendation. Much more important than individual values are ratios." • "The very most important numbers are (namely) those that are not in a report or on a presentation slide, but that you derive yourself. By seemingly conjuring up these numbers …, you differentiate yourself from ninety percent of all careerists. Someone who can 'read between the lines' stands out."

Table: Tips and tricks for a "Crazy career" according to Schur and Weick (2005), freely translated

There is little to be said against these techniques, perhaps only the following: Mahan Khalsa has pointed out that customers accept business cases primarily when we have received the underlying figures from them or developed them together with them (Khalsa 1999). Additionally, we should be clear about our calculation method, otherwise the cleverness becomes a boomerang. The most important single number is still "42" (Adams 2000).

Tips & Tricks	Comment / Quotation
Important techniques **Questions**	• "He who asks, leads!" … "Well-asked questions are the key to many things. They create downward pressure, demonstrate overview and intelligence, and can make competitors break out in a cold sweat. Ultimately, they also distract from your own weaknesses. There are few instruments of power that are more effective than targeted questions. And none that can be used so well at all levels of the hierarchy." • "The most important basic rule is not to ask closed questions and, if possible, not to ask obvious questions." … "Questions that offer alternatives are also bad." … "Lead your counterpart into territory where he feels uncomfortable or at least unsure." … "Constantly drive him forward with open-ended 'W' questions (Who? Why? When? …)." … "Never be satisfied with the first answers! Ask for more! Drill deeper. It's worth it. Questions are like probing fingers in an open wound. And use pauses. Deadly pauses."

Table: Tips and tricks for a "Crazy career" according to Schur and Weick (2005), freely translated

Comment: These career tips are aimed at the careerist who wants to outdo his opponents or shine in front of his superiors. This is, of course, the opposite of Level 5 leadership or the Fifteen Commitments (see below for leadership success). Of course, the W-questions also have their substantive merits. For example, Kenichi Ohmae suggests asking **"Why?"** until the respondent is annoyed (but the problem is truly understood) (Ohmae 1985). This is along the lines of the **Ishikawa diagram** (fishbone analysis) and is done, however, in the spirit of constructive resolution, not to humiliate a counterpart.

Tips & Tricks	Comment / Quotation
Important techniques **Breaks**	• "Junior staff are trained how to talk properly. But it would be much more important to learn how to be silent properly! And that means in conversations. This seems counterintuitive, but it's not. When two or more people sit together and the conversation rests for a while, a tremendous amount happens. This 'doing nothing' and 'saying nothing' develops a huge power. Nothing can come close to that power, no matter how brilliant the argument." • "Pauses have something in common with good questions: they use your counterpart's intellect and knowledge against themselves. Those who are asked know that a certain answer is expected of them. Those who are not addressed know nothing at all. Pauses leave the communication level and push massively onto the relationship level. With unheard-of brutality. There is little that makes a person more insecure ... And because very few people can tolerate that, they blurt something out in such situations. And with that, they've lost."

Table: Tips and tricks for a "Crazy career" according to Schur and Weick (2005), freely translated

Other management schools propagate the absolute opposite: **"Nonviolent communication"**, an approach developed by Marshal Rosenberg (Rosenberg 2012). In addition, Schur and Weick **emphasize the importance of role models, mentors and coaches for success** and good appearance. Furthermore, **"Pretty people get an attractiveness bonus** (about 10%) and ugly people get an ugliness penalty (between -5 and -10%) in the same position" (Schur and Weick 2005). They also emphasize the necessity of having enemies. After all, if you don't have enemies, you don't matter to them. Of course, you can have a different opinion about this. Schur and Weick additionally have a clear opinion about the influence of luck and chance: Comparable to the example of Lincoln (Nagler 2015), **one should never leave anything to chance if one could influence it oneself**. Schur and Weick also point out the **dangers of staying abroad**. As long as you **stay in the "center of power"**, it's harmless. Otherwise, a stay abroad can be a terrible professional dead end and slow you down while your competitors pass you by careerwise.

The **qualities** highlighted by Schur and Weick **for top managers** (this is not a big surprise) are the following: **mental flexibility, intelligence, creativity, sense of priorities, decisiveness, willingness to deal with conflict** and, above all, **courage**. These are all qualities that Sunzi, Musashi, Machiavelli, Clausewitz or Covey, Drucker and Collins could also demand. In addition to their tips, Schur and Weick also set out a number of **rules for career success**. Some will sound quite familiar or compelling to you, such as **delegating properly**, **not relying on the HRM department** alone (anything else would also be naive), or **being good with people**. Other rules might alienate you: e.g., "Be unfair" or only dealing WITH ("Being good with") people but not being good TO people; even the **advice to be disloyal** or to **start many things but not deliver**. However, the success of some politicians seems to prove Schur and Weick – unfortunately – right (e.g., changing positions and leaving key projects and initiatives early and then blaming the successor; not completing studies, etc.). Your customers, but also all the entrepreneurs or intrapreneurs will have a completely different opinion on the subject of delivery (they need the results!). We also take a more differentiated view of the thesis regarding **rule violations**. The well-known career counselor Heiko Mell would claim that major rule violations are definitely and usually punished quite severely. It depends!

Rule	Thesis / Concept
1	Never work with computers yourself!
2	Intentionally unlearn what you know
3	Be in the center of power …, not where the work is done
4	Never rely on the human resource department
5	Be good with people
6	Deliberately break rules
7	Always get the support of powerful people in critical situations
8	Start many things, but don't finish anything substantial
9	Career and company interests have nothing to do with each other
10	Demonstrate slavish obedience
11	Be unforgiving and – if necessary – unfair
12	Never share success in the presence of important people
13	Make a mountain out of a molehill
14	Do not be loyal
15	Never be consistent – change your mind every day
16	Consider your family as an "appendix / appenage" of your career
17	When you are on top, ask yourself one question (what for / why?)

Table: Rules for a "Crazy career" (Schur and Weick 2005), freely translated

Remark: Mell has published several notable books and weekly articles in VDI nachrichten on career advice in industry over the past few decades. These are good sources to gain useful complementary insights and should be taken into account.

	The ten most important "system-immanent" basic rules for success at work	Our interpretation
1	Keep your qualification "marketable".	Secure your market value through lifelong learning.
2	The company's goal is not to employ people.	Be aware of the company's main objectives and understand them.
3	Companies strive for successful advancement, and the employee who best fits that goal strives for a successful career.	Be aware of the company's main objectives and provide appropriate added value.

	The ten most important "system-immanent" basic rules for success at work	Our interpretation
4	The employee is a dependent employee. Thus, there are limits to the free development of his personality.	Recognize the reality and dependencies you have as an employee. Act accordingly.
5	A good employee is someone whom his boss considers to be so.	See Khalsa: "Helping clients succeed"; replace "client" with "boss".
6	The successful hunter only has his cave where the mammoths are. Even today, "mammoths," i.e., jobs that fit the demanding career goals of academics, are by no means coincidentally always where the "hunter" has his current residence; here, a willingness to change is often required.	Be flexible and open for change; remain locally unbound.
7	The "Mell's priority list" (only one topic per rank)	Set priorities with a clear order.
8	Manage yourself as if you were your own small company.	Think like an entrepreneur and act accordingly (think of your market value).
9	Supervisors expect performance and respect from their employees. Boss criticism is like the tip of an iceberg.	Meet your manager's expectations in a respectful manner. Build a good relationship with them.
10	Personality is more important for a career than purely technical ability.	Knowledge and expertise alone are not enough.

Table: The ten most important "system-immanent" basic rules for success at work (Mell 2023), freely translated

At the end of their business novel, Schur and Weick pose the **question of meaning** and **what for** (including the impact on your personal life, environment and family). And it should be clear: Sooner or later, each of us will certainly ask ourselves the question of the meaning of life (also and especially in the context of an impressive career). We therefore recommend reading the **"Self-Reflections"** of the emperor Marcus Aurelius or the profound works of **Victor Frankl** (Marc Aurel 2019, Frankl 2019 and 2020). And it is your sole responsibility to find a satisfactory answer.

Success Through the Application of Stratagems

"When everybody looks right, you go left" (Bruce Willis aka Mr. Goodkat on the deception and diversionary "Kansas City Shuffle" in the movie "Lucky Number Slevin" (2006) by Paul McGuigan); see also stratagem No. 6.

"(1) If it is not proper, do not do it. If it is not true, then do not say it. (2) For your endeavor shall be upright" (Marcus Aurelius in his Self-Reflections – Twelfth Book, 17, freely translated).

When dealing with success in career, one insight can be gained: The use of tricks or lists can benefit us. The tricks and lists of our opponents (e.g., competitors, companies), on the other hand, can harm us. Think of the cunning Ulysses (e.g., the Trojan horse) or Prometheus who outwitted Zeus. So, we should be on our guard. Applying lists and protecting ourselves from them is a strategic or implementation issue. Think of Hannibal's march across the Alps or Manstein's sickle-cut plan. Don't forget Ray Kroc, the so-called "Hamburger King" and CEO of McDonald's Corporation (The Founder 2016) or Dr. Michael Burry, who bet against the U.S. real estate market (The Big Short 2015), see also Glossary. It seems so important to us that we want to consider it separately here. The well-known stratagem researcher Harro von Senger summarizes his findings as follows (Senger 2016a and 2016b):

"Europeans find it difficult to use a ruse. Either they consider cunning behavior reprehensible from the outset, or they plan their cunning so half-heartedly that it is immediately seen through. It is often considered indelicate to analyze the behavior of others with regard to possible tricks. In China, however, seeing through and using cunning has been highly valued and cultivated since ancient times. China is the only civilization in the world to have named and systematically compiled various techniques of outwitting. It is important to learn from this catalog of 36 stratagems, which was kept secret for centuries" (Senger 2016a, freely translated). Remark: Senger points out that Clausewitz underestimated the issue of cunning in war. Clausewitz described cunning as a kind of weakness or sign of despair, see Chapter X in "Vom Kriege" (see also Senger 2016a and Ritter 2022). Cf. Madden (2022): "Operation Mincemeat saved tens of thousands of lives. It is now celebrated as the most spectacular single episode in the history of deception. The invasion of Sicily was a triumph. It was a definitive moment in the fight against Hitler and a crucial step towards Allied victory in Europe".

Of course, the use of lists is not a Chinese invention, as a look at history shows.

"... From this it is easy to see that a general must never trust in an obvious mistake of the enemy, for there will always be a trick behind it, because men cannot reasonably be so careless" (Machiavelli in the Discorsi, 3rd book, 48th chapter, freely translated).

"(8) Then, what is bad and strange about a boor acting like a boor? See if you don't rather blame yourself because you didn't expect him to commit this transgression. (9) You also had the ability to consider from your reason that he would probably commit this mistake, and yet you did not think about it and are now surprised when he has committed a mistake" (Marcus Aurelius in his Self-Reflections – Ninth Book, 42 (8 – 9), freely translated).

However, Senger may be right in that **stratagems** are treated much more systematically in Chinese culture. According to the German "Duden" (i.e., a dictionary of the Standard High German language), cunning is first of all a clever means by which one tries to achieve something that cannot be achieved in the normal way. In other words, **an unorthodox, unexpected solution**. Let's take a quick look at what we call the **36 stratagems**. We recommend reading the noteworthy books by Senger, who looks at the topic from different perspectives (e.g., personal success, management, and protection from stratagems, see Senger 2016a and 2016b and tables below).

	Thirty-Six Stratagems	
1	**Deceiving the Heaven to cross the sea / Deceiving the emperor** (by inviting him to a house on the seashore that is actually a disguised ship) and (thus cause him to) cross the sea (i.e., target camouflage, signal falsification, course disguise, stealth stratagem, coram publico stratagem).	
2	**Lay siege to** (the unprotected capital of) **Wei in order to save** (the state of) **Zhao**, which is under attack by the main force of Wei (i.e., thrust-into-void stratagem, Achilles heel stratagem – indirect defeat of the opponent by threatening one of his unprotected weak points).	
3	**Killing with another's knife** (i.e., straw man or proxy stratagem – eliminating the opponent at someone else's hands. Alibi or desk offender stratagem – harming someone in an indirect way without exposing oneself).	

	Thirty-Six Stratagems
4	**Expecting the exhausted enemy when rested** (i.e., stratagem of sitting out; stratagem of exhaustion). Comment: probably the only stratagem formulated by Sunzi (cunning is only one aspect for Master Sun).
5	**Exploit a conflagration for a robbery** (i.e., vulture stratagem; emergency exploitation stratagem – to take advantage of another's distress, difficulties, crisis).
6	**Make noise in the east, attack in the west** (i.e., in an ancestral sense attack target stratagem or in a more general sense distraction stratagem)
7	**Create something out of nothing** (i.e., creator stratagem – gaining advantage by pretending to be a mirage or outplaying the opponent thanks to a new constructive idea).
8	**Visibly repairing the** (burned) **boardwalks, secretly** (but before finished repair) **marching to Chencang** (to attack the opponent) (i.e., stratagem of veiled marching direction or second way and detour stratagem as well as normality stratagem).
9	(Seemingly uninvolved) **observe the conflagration on the opposite shore** (i.e., stratagem of non-intervention; wait-and-see stratagem).
10	**Hide the dagger behind the smile** (i.e., duplicity stratagem and Janus head stratagem; lulling and Judas kiss stratagem).
11	**Withering the plum tree instead of the peach tree** (i.e., scapegoat / sacrificial lamb stratagem; pawn sacrifice / lady sacrifice stratagem).
12	**To lead away with a light hand the sheep** (which unexpectedly crosses one's path) (i.e., additional chances stratagem; kairos stratagem; serendipity stratagem – constant and all-round readiness to exploit chances to gain an advantage – "staging chance").
13	**Striking on the grass to flush out the snakes** (i.e., trial balloon / test run stratagem; indirect deterrence stratagem; warning shot stratagem; provocation stratagem).
14	**Borrow a corpse for the return of the soul** (i.e., re-novation stratagem; warm-up stratagem; patina stratagem – "old wine in new wineskins").
15	**Lure the tiger from the mountain to the plain** (i.e., isolation stratagem – separate the opponent from his base / from his most important helpers).
16	**If you want to catch something, you have to let it go first** (i.e., laissez-faire stratagem).
17	**Throw a brick to get a jade stone** (i.e., bait stratagem – make a big profit with an insignificant gift).
18	**If you want to disarm a band of robbers, you have to catch their leader** (i.e., leader-capture stratagem; head-butt stratagem).
19	**To secretly pull away the firewood from under the kettle** (i.e., root-elimination stratagem; force-drawing or conflict-dampening stratagem).
20	**To cloud the water in order to catch the fish** (deprived of their clear vision) (i.e., cloudy stratagem; confusion stratagem; chaos stratagem).

	Thirty-Six Stratagems
21	**The cicada slips out of its golden shining shell** (i.e., desecration stratagem; change of shape / metamorphosis stratagem).
22	**Close the door and catch the thief** (i.e., encirclement stratagem).
23	**Ally with the distant enemy to attack the near enemy** (i.e., temporary distant friendship / temporary distant alliance stratagem; annihilation alliance stratagem; hegemony stratagem).
24	**Borrowing a way** (through the state of Yu) **for an attack against** (its neighboring state) **Guo** (to conquer Yu after occupying Guo) (i.e., two-step stratagem, double-target stratagem as well as end-goal concealment – letting someone dig his own grave without him realizing it).
25	(Without changing the facade of a house inside) **steal the supporting beams and replace the supporting posts** (i.e., removal stratagem).
26	**Scold the acacia tree, but point at the mulberry tree** (i.e., stratagem of indirect criticism; shadow boxing stratagem; stratagem of indirect aggression).
27	**Mime craziness without losing balance** (i.e., fool, greenhorn, or Till Eulenspiegel stratagem).
28	**Lure onto the roof, then pull away the ladder** (i.e., deadlock stratagem; dead-end stratagem; exit-prevention stratagem).
29	**Decorate a** (scrawny) **tree with** (artificial) **flowers** (i.e., stratagem of pretending, imitating, or making up stratagem; Potemkin villages stratagem).
30	**Reversing the role of the guest to that of the host** (i.e., stratagem of unnoticed power position theft; infiltration stratagem; cuckoo's stratagem; power usurpation stratagem).
31	**The stratagem of the beautiful man / woman** (i.e., Adonis / Venus trap; sex, decoy stratagem; corrupting stratagem).
32	**The stratagem of opening the gates** (of a city in reality not ready for defense; i.e., stratagem of feigned ambush / risk; warning stratagem; all-clear stratagem).
33	**The agent stratagem / stratagem of sowing discord** (i.e., infiltration stratagem; agent-provocateur stratagem; destabilization stratagem).
34	**The stratagem of suffering flesh / stratagem of self-mutilation** (i.e., alleged defector stratagem; victim status stratagem; compassion stratagem; self-flagellation stratagem; pardon stratagem; Canossa stratagem).
35	**The concatenation stratagem** (i.e., entanglement stratagem; connection stratagem (mainly opposite things); stratagem chaining (simultaneous or successive)).
36	(Timely) **running away is the best thing to do** (when complete hopelessness becomes obvious) (i.e., retreat stratagem; change of course stratagem; escape stratagem; distance gaining stratagem).

Table: The 36 Stratagems according to Harro von Senger (2016a und 2016b), see also
36 Stratagems – the Secret Book of the Art of War" (ca. 1500 A.D.), freely translated

	Six categories of cunning techniques	
1	Cover-up stratagems (concealment of a reality that actually exists, or rather, one withdraws it from view) **(DECEPTION-STRATAGEMS)**	Assignment: stratagems 1, 3, 6, 8, 10, 24, 25
2	Pretense-stratagems – simulation-strategems (one pretends a non-existing reality) **(DECEPTION-STRATAGEMS)**	Assignment: stratagems 7, 27, 29, 32, 34
3	Revealing stratagems – information stratagems (one conveys or reveals an unknown reality) **(PRESENCE-STRATAGEMS)**	Assignment: stratagems 13, 26
4	Exploitation stratagems (one takes advantage of a favorable constellation that has temporarily arisen or otherwise exists without having done anything to bring it about) **(PRESENCE-STRATAGEMS)**	Assignment: stratagems 2, 4, 5, 12, 14, 15, 16, 17, 18, 19, 20, 22, 23, 28, 30, 31, 33 Comment: Senger counts stratagem 9 in "The Art of Cunning" as one of the exploitations stratagems.
5	Stratagem chaining (one applies, usually one after the other, two or more stratagems to achieve a goal) **(PRESENCE-STRATAGEMS)**	Assignment: stratagem 35
6	Escape stratagems (one escapes from a precarious reality) **(STRATAGEM-MIX)**	Assignment: stratagems 9, 11, 21, 36
(7)	Hybrid stratagems (one performs an action that can be simultaneously assigned to stratagems of different basic categories; dissimulation thus goes hand in hand with simulation) **(STRATAGEM-MIX)**	Comment: In "The Art of Cunning" Harro von Senger originally distinguishes seven basic categories of stratagems. In contrast to six categories in "36 Stratagems for Managers" which also takes into account the (Chinese) idea of symmetry (6x6=36).

Table: Six categories of list techniques according to Harro von Senger (2016b), freely translated

		Four ethical categories of cunning
1	**Damage stratagems**	The destructive, egoistic moment predominates. Example: the stratagems of economic criminals.
2	**Service stratagems**	They are directed towards constructive goals. Example: the mental-present application of the kairos stratagem No. 12 (recognizing and exploiting business opportunities).
3	**Joke stratagems**	Here cunning is used for amusement. Example: joke articles in the assortment of goods. In business, joke stratagems seem to be hardly recognized and exploited, especially in the area of advertising, which is generally far too serious.
4	**Ethical hybrid stratagems**	Here one does not know whether the destructive prevails, whether one should laugh or cry. Example: certain Benetton advertising campaigns, which caused a sensation and were successful in this respect, but which made one feel uncomfortable.

Table: Four ethical categories of cunning according to Harro von Senger (2016b), freely translated

"... Only this I want to say, that I do not think of considering as glorious every fraud that you commit by breaking words and contracts. This may sometimes help you to land and dominion, but it will never bring you glory. I am speaking here only of the deceit by which you deceive the enemy who does not trust you, and on which, in fact, the art of war is based" (Machiavelli in the Discorsi, 3rd book, 40th chapter, freely translated).

To be successful, the use of stratagems can be promising. But how can we protect ourselves? We need to **develop a sensor for stratagems** or list sensitivity **("Strategemische Wachsamkeit").**

	Procedure/Approach – Stra-Wach (strategemische Wachsamkeit, i.e., stratagemic vigilance)
1	Rough stratagem analysis (not only actions of the counterpart that are suspicious of stratagems): a) Is the situation conducive to deception (deception situation) or does it favor skillful reality shaping (presence situation)? b) In the case of a deception situation: Is there evidence that something is being faked or concealed? c) In the case of a presence situation: Is something being exploited, detected, or is an escape from something being taken? d) Is it a stratagemically complex situation or procedure?

	Procedure/Approach – Stra-Wach (strategemische Wachsamkeit, i.e., stratagemic vigilance)
2	Stratagemic detailed analysis with the help of the catalog of 36 stratagems
3	Stratagemic self-analysis (own actions, also completely unstratagemic ones) under the aspects of provocation of our counterpart and possible reactions: a) Can our counterpart use, e.g., concealment stratagems like No. 25 against us? b) Can our opponent use, e.g., exploitation stratagems like No. 12, 17, 19, 20, 30, 31 or 33 against us? Comment: "For every stupid thing there is a person who commits it!"

Table: "How to see through a ruse?" according to Harro von Senger (2016a), freely translated

Knowing our enemy, their stratagems and **protecting against them** is important.

"However, we should always be guided by the advice of the Chinese sage Hong Zicheng from the Ming period (1368–1644): 'One must not have a heart that harms people! But a heart taking care of people is indispensable!'" (Senger 2016a, freely translated).

"I am sending you out like sheep among wolves. Therefore, be as shrewd as snakes and as innocent as doves" (Matthew 10:16, New International Version, (https://www.biblegateway.com/passage/?search=Matthew%2010%3A16&version=NIV (Status: August 2024)).

Consulting Success

"Helping people and organizations achieve what is important to them in a way they feel good about it. It is a paradigm, mental model, or frame of reference for how consultants work efficiently with clients" (Khalsa 1999).

As mentioned earlier, Covey recommends finding a win/win situation ("Think Win/Win", see Habit 4, see page 41). This is quite different from the career tips of Schur and Weick, as we have already seen. Mahan Khalsa, a follower of the Covey community, on the other hand, goes even one step further: **We will only be successful if we make our customer successful** (Khalsa 1999). This statement means much more than the familiar marketing slogan "Fulfill or exceed customer expectation" (Jobber 2001). Let us now take a brief look at "Helping clients succeed" (Khalsa 1999).

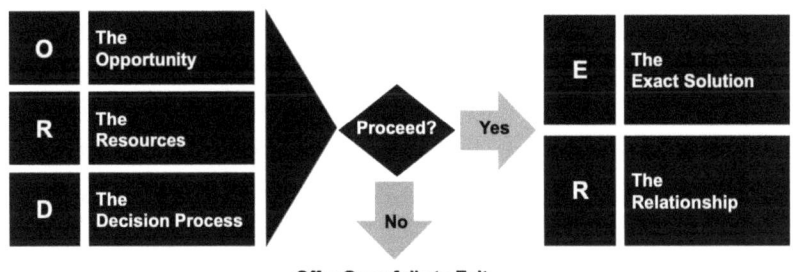

Figure: The ORDER principle according to Khalsa (1999). The "O-R-D" of the Khalsa solution approach corresponds to the acquisition phase; the "E" then to the actual project phase. The decisive factor for sustainable success is then the "R": the development of a sustainable, trusting and long-term relationship.

ORDER model according to Khalsa: "Helping clients succeed"	
Opportunity	Develop mutually a sound business case or discover that a solution does not exist
Resources	Congruence in time, people and money
Decision process	Gain mutually clarity about decision steps and decisions/criteria (when, who and how)
Exact Solution	Give evidence and proof to resolve client's problem according to available resources and to matches with decision criteria
Relationship	Create positive and ongoing relationship

Table: The ORDER principle according to Khalsa (1999)

The ORDER principle in a nutshell:

- Find out: What is **the real problem (pain)** or **opportunity (gain)**? We have to understand this in any case.
- Then there is what Khalsa calls the **evidence of the problem or opportunity**. The customer has to be really sure himself and be able to prove that there is a problem or an opportunity. Of course, this includes clarity about the respective boundary conditions, the context or the "impacts" of a change. The same also applies to the case: What if nothing changes or nothing improves? How great is the suffering, the pain?
- What is the associated **business case**? Only if there is a business case or a **need** at all is it even worth solving the problem.
- Does the customer **know the business case** or does he trust the available figures from it? Mahan Khalsa rightly points out that **only a business case that comes from the customer or was developed together with the customer is at all convincing for the customer**. If we have developed it together with the customer, the acceptance of the presented figures, such as cost-benefit or expected cash flows, is quite high. If it only comes from us, he will probably distrust our

figures, even if they are completely correct! And don't forget: NPV is a type of guessing as we make assumptions about the future discount rate and future cash flows. In the end, however, these are merely assumptions. Our advice: It is therefore better to make decisions on the basis of several scenarios.

- On top of that, we need to **gain clarity about the available needed resources**, such as available time, money and contacts, supporters, etc. It is quite possible that there might very well be a really good business case, but a potential project might not start until next year, when the required staff will be fully available again or the budget is available or can be made available due to next year's planning. So even if we find out, for example, that the customer has all the resources except the budget, that doesn't have to be a fundamental show stopper. Perhaps we could start a preliminary or sub-project together fairly soon and then the budget needed is available at a later date.

- And we should never forget that: We need to **know the decision-making process and the decision-making criteria** in the company or organization. The person responsible for the problem, the decision maker and the person responsible for the budget can be different people (this is the normal case). Furthermore, Khalsa recommends: Please **try to present** the final offer **PERSONALLY** to the decision makers if possible. This is your last chance to influence a decision.

Remark: The ORDER principle is a very suitable concept for consulting and suppliers. Moreover, **you can apply the same ideas in your own organization. Treat your bosses like customers**. This concept can really help you advance your career.

Leadership Success

We have quoted Henry Mintzberg regarding the "one best way" of organizations and strategies. Maybe it sounds banal, but we could come to the same conclusion regarding management and leadership. Leadership success is essential for the survival of organizations. According to Dethmer, Chapman and Warner Klemp, we can distinguish four ways of leading.

TO ME – LIFE HAPPENS TO ME	
Posture	Victim
Experience	Blaming and complaining
Beliefs	There is a problem. Someone is at fault. Someone should fix it.
Key questions	Why me? Whose fault it is?
Benefits	Experience separateness; defined identity, entertaining drama; supports empathy, adrenaline high
BY ME – I MAKE LIFE HAPPEN	
Posture	Creator
Experience	Appreciation
Beliefs	Problems are here for me to learn from. I create the problem, so I can solve it.
Key questions	What can I learn? What do I want to create?
Benefits	Personal empowerment; define your wants and desires
THROUGH ME – I COOPERATE WITH LIFE HAPPENING	
Posture	Co-creator
Experience	Allowing, flow, wonder and awe
Beliefs	I am the source of all meaning. I experience things as perfect, whole and complete. Life handles all apparent "problems".
Key questions	What wants to happen through me?
Benefits	Non-attachment; unlimited possibility; plenty of everything
AS ME – LIFE IS ME	
Posture	At one with all
Experience	Peace, spaciousness
Beliefs	There is just openness. There are no problems, and no one to "solve" them.
Key questions	No more questions – just knowingness
Benefits	Experience oneness & non-dualism; unlimited freedom & peace

Table: Four Ways of Leading according to Dethmer et al. (2015)

Each leadership style comes with some advantages and disadvantages. Also, each style must fit you, your personality, your organization, and your culture (Think Strategic fit). The "AS ME – LIFE IS ME" style is more appropriate for religious leaders like Buddha. Note: Dethmer, Chapman and Warner Klemp are followers of Gay Hendricks. Even if you don't share their key concepts, however, it's worth taking a quick look at what they call "The 15 Commitments of Conscious Leadership: A New Paradigm for Sustainable Success", see next table.

Commitment "above the line" versus "below the line"			
1	Taking radical responsi- bility	I commit to taking full responsibility for the circum- stances of my life and for my physical, emotional, mental, and spiritual well- being. I commit to support- ing others to take full responsibility for their lives.	I commit to blaming others and myself for what is wrong in the world. I commit to being a victim, villain or a hero and taking more or less than 100 percent responsibility.
2	Learning Through Curiosity	I commit to growing in self- awareness. I commit to regarding every interaction as an opportunity to learn. I commit to curiosity as a path to rapid learning.	I commit to being right and seeing this situation as something that is happening to me. I commit to being defensive, especially when I am certain that I am RIGHT.
3	Feeling all Feelings	I commit to feeling my feelings all the way through to completion. They come, and I locate them in my body then move, breathe, and vocalize them so they release all the way through.	I commit to resisting, judging and apologizing for my feelings. I repress, avoid, and withhold them.
4	Speaking Candidly	I commit to saying what is true for me. I commit to being a person to whom others can express them- selves with candor.	I commit to withholding my truth (facts, feelings, things I imagine) and speaking in a way that allows me to try to manipulate an outcome. I commit to not listening to the other person.
5	Eliminating Gossip	I commit to ending gossip, talking directly to people with whom I have a con- cern, and encouraging	I commit to saying things about people that I would not or will not say to them. I com- mit to talking about people in

		Commitment "above the line" versus "below the line"	
		others to talk directly to people with whom they have an issue or concern.	ways I wouldn't if they were in the room. I commit to listening to others when they gossip.
6	Practicing Integrity	I commit to the masterful practice of integrity, including acknowledging all authentic feelings, expressing the unarguable truth, keeping my agreements, and taking 100 percent responsibility.	I commit to living in incompletion by withholding my truth, denying my feelings, not keeping my agreements, and not taking 100 percent responsibility.
7	Generating Appreciation	I commit to living in appreciation, fully opening to both receiving and giving appreciation.	I commit to feeling entitled to 'what's mine' resenting when it's not acknowledged in the way I want.
8	Excelling in Your Zone of Genius	I commit to expressing my full magnificence and to supporting and inspiring others to fully express their creativity and live in their zone of genius.	I commit to holding myself back and not realizing my full potential by living in areas of incompetence, competence, and even excellence.
9	Living a Life of Play and Rest	I commit to creating a life of play, improvisation, and laughter. I commit to seeing all of life unfold easefully, and effortlessly. I commit to maximizing my energy by honoring rest, renewal, and rhythm.	I commit to seeing my life as serious: it requires hard work, effort, and struggle. I see play and rest as distractions from effectiveness and efficiency.
10	Exploring the Opposite	I commit to seeing that the opposite of my story is as true as or truer than my original story. I recognize that I interpret the world around me and give my stories meaning.	I commit to believing my stories and the meaning I give them as the truth.
11	Sourcing Approval, Control and Security	I commit to being the source of my approval, control and security.	I commit to living from the belief that my approval, control, and security come from the outside – from people, circumstances, and conditions.
12	Having Enough of	I commit to experiencing that I have enough of everything ... including time,	I commit to a scarcity mentality choosing to see that there is 'not enough' for me and

Commitment "above the line" versus "below the line"			
	Every-thing	money, love, energy, space, resources, etc.	others in the world and therefore I have to be conscious of making sure I get and preserve what is 'mine'.
13	**Experienc-ing the World as an Ally**	I commit to seeing all people and circumstances as allies that are perfectly suited to help me learn the most important things for my growth.	I commit to seeing other people and circumstances as obstacles and impediments to getting what I most want.
14	**Creating Win for ALL Solutions**	I commit to creating win-for-all solutions (win for me, win for the other person, win for the organization, and win for the whole) for whatever issues, problems, concerns, or opportunities life gives me.	I commit to seeing life as a zero-sum game, creating win/lose solutions for whatever issues, problems, concerns, or opportunities life gives me.
15	**Being the Resolution**	I commit to being the resolution or solution that is needed: seeing what is missing in the world as an invitation to become that which is required.	I commit to responding to the needs of the world with apathy or resentment and doing nothing or assigning blame to others.

Table: "The 15 Commitments of Conscious Leadership: A new paradigm for sustainable success" according to Dethmer et al. (2015) – see also Hendricks (2009)

As announced when we talked about effectiveness as a key success factor, let's now share the insights **Peter Drucker** gained in the context of **"Effective Executives"**. Professor Peter Ferdinand Drucker is also called the "father of modern management" by Philip Kotler. This thought probably amused Drucker himself very much, as Fredmund Malik wrote in the preface to "The Effective Executive: Gaining Effectiveness and Ability to Act in the Leadership Role": "if anyone invented management at all, it was perhaps rather the CEO of the company 'Cheops GmbH' in pharaonic Egypt, which had 30,000 workers on its construction sites ..." Drucker's work is extraordinary and quite extensive (Drucker 2014a and 2014b), see "Management by

Objectives", the "Concept of Core Competence", the "Knowledge Worker" or "The Effective Executive".

"Effective leaders have a wide variety of character traits, strengths, weaknesses, values and views. **Their only commonality is that they do the right things.** Some are born to be effective. But the need is far too great to be met by outstanding talent alone. Effectiveness is a discipline. And like any discipline, effectiveness can be learned and must be worked at" (Drucker 2014b, freely translated).

The Effective Executive – Eight (or Nine) Virtues of Being a Leader		
	Virtue (of effective executives)	Objective / Findings
1	They asked themselves: **"What needs to be done?"**	**What actions need to be taken?**
2	They asked themselves: **"What is right for the company?"**	
3	They developed **action plans.**	**Effective implementation of knowledge**
4	They took **responsibility for** their **decisions.**	
5	They took **responsibility for** their **communications.**	
6	They **focused on opportunities** rather than problems.	
7	They made sure their meetings were **productive meetings.**	**Ensuring that the entire organization feels responsible and accountable for implementation**
8	They didn't **think and say** "I" but **"we".**	
(9)	**"Listen and don't speak until everything has been said."**	**Rule (Drucker's personal advice)**

Table: Lessons from "The Effective Executive" according to Drucker (2014), freely translated

Important rules for setting priorities	
1	**Give priority to the future over the past**
2	**Focus on opportunities and not on problems**
3	**Go your own way instead of just jumping on a running train**
4	**Set high goals that really make a difference, instead of just aiming for something that is safe and easy to accomplish**

Table: Courage is needed, not analytical procedures – lessons from "The Effective Executive" according to Drucker (2014), freely translated. 1.) Cf. Machiavelli in "Il Principe", 2.) Cf. Collins and Porras (2004) and Collins (2020) as well as Big Hairy Audacious Goals (BHAG).

"Those who make a focused effort to productively use existing strengths in themselves and others simultaneously help to make organizational performance capability compatible with personal success and actively turn their own knowledge into an opportunity for the entire organization" (Drucker 2014b, freely translated).

	There are essentially five practices, five mental habits that must be adopted to become effective as a leader:
1	Effective leaders **know what they spend their time on**. They work systematically to allocate what little time they can under their control wisely.
2	Effective leaders **focus on making an outward contribution**. They focus their efforts more on results than on the work itself. The starting point for them is not the work that needs to be done, let alone the techniques and tools required, but rather the question, **"What results are expected of me?"**
3	Effective leaders **build on strengths** – their own strengths, the strengths of their supervisors, peers and subordinates; and on the "strengths" of the situation, that is, what they can do. **They don't build on weaknesses. They don't start with things they can't do.**
4	Effective leaders **focus on a few big areas where outstanding performance leads to great results**. They force themselves to **prioritize** and **stick to their decision-making**. They know they have no choice but to **do first things first** – and **not do second things at all**. The only alternative is to get no results at all.
5	Last but not least, effective leaders **make effective decisions**. They know that this is primarily a matter of having the right system – that is, **the right steps in the right order**. They know that an effective decision is always based on a **weighing of different opinions**, not on a consensus of facts. And they also know that if you make a lot of decisions quickly, you make the wrong decisions. **What is needed are few, but fundamental decisions. What's needed is the right strategy – not effective tactics without substance.**

Table: Lessons from "The Effective Executive" according to Drucker (2014), freely translated. See also the example of Lincoln (Nagler 2015) and Moltke (Möbius and Bigge 2023)

Management expert Jim Collins provides some complementary insights to Stephen Covey and Peter Drucker, see **"Good to Great: Why Some Companies Make the Leap and Others Don't"** and **"Built to Last: Successful Habits of Visionary Companies"** (Collins 2020, Collins and Porras 2004). A key element is **"Level 5 leadership"**, see tables below.

"Level 5 leadership qualities ... a paradoxical blend of humility, as far as the person is concerned, and professional willpower in all matters of business. They are more reminiscent of Lincoln or Socrates than of General Patton or Caesar" (Collins 2020, freely translated).

Level 5 hierarchy – The five levels of individual leadership competence		
Level 5	Level 5 leader	Ensures sustainable top performance through a paradoxical mixture of personal modesty and professional assertiveness.
Level 4	Effective manager	Ensures commitment and consistent implementation of a clear and compelling vision; stimulates higher standards of performance.
Level 3	Competent manager	Organizes people and resources for effective and efficient implementation of set goals.
Level 2	Team member	Contributes individual skills to the success of group goals and works effectively with others in a group.
Level 1	Talented individuum	Makes productive contributions through talent, knowledge, skills and good work habits.

Table: "Level 5 hierarchy – The five levels of individual leadership" according to Collins (2020), freely translated

The two sides of Level 5 leadership – Summary	
Professional determination	**Personal modesty**
Ensures top results; acts as a key catalyst for business turnaround.	Unobtrusive appearance; shuns public praise; refrains from any form of boasting.
Demonstrates consistent determination; does what must be done to produce long-term top results, no matter how difficult.	Acts calmly but firmly; motivates not by personal charisma but by outstanding standards.
Sets the standard for building a lasting top company and does not settle for less.	Puts all ambition into the service of the company, not his ego; selects successors who will make the company even more successful in the future.
Looks in the mirror, not out the window, to find the person responsible for poor results; never blames others or blames external factors; never talks about bad luck.	Looks out the window, not in the mirror, to explain company successes; finds reasons in colleagues, external factors, luck.

Table: Level 5 hierarchy according to Collins (2020), freely translated

In a nutshell, a Level 5 leader is someone who is in no way inferior to an Elon Musk, Jack Ma, Jeff Bezos, Warren Buffet, Bill Gates or Steve Jobs **in terms of ambition, energy, diligence, willpower** and other qualities. The big difference with some of these candidates, however, is that they don't take themselves too seriously personally and subordinate all their ambition and energy to the success of their company (or organization or country; see also the example of Lincoln or Moltke) and align everything else accordingly. Basically, they don't follow Schur and Weick's self-serving career tips (completely). Furthermore, Level 5 leadership is based on a **Culture of discipline** (the details are explained in the next chapter).

Disciplined People	
1	Level 5 leadership
2	First who, then what
Disciplined Thought	
3	Confront the brutal facts
4	Hedgehog concept – Three overlapping circles
Disciplined Action	
5	Culture of discipline
6	Technology accelerators
Turn upon turn, building momentum until a point of breakthrough, and beyond	
7	Flywheel

Table: One culture of discipline – "Good to Great" according to Collins (2020), freely translated

We will quickly come back to Collins when we talk about business success in a moment. In the context of leadership, we should not forget Moltke and his military style of leading, **"Auftragstaktik"** (i.e., "Mission command", or "Führen durch Auftrag", i.e., **"Leading by mission"**): the (military) leader specifies the objective, usually the time frame and the required forces. On the basis of these framework conditions, the leader tasked with the mission pursues and achieves the objective independently and flexibly. This approach is much more powerful than agile management. This concept has been successfully applied in management, too (e.g., "Planned opportunism", a concept developed by Jack Welsh, a fan of Moltke) or is align with the ideas of Peter Drucker (Management by objectives). In addition, as Chief of Staff of the Prussian Army, Moltke, a student of Clausewitz, further developed strategy along the lines of Scharnhorst, Gneisenau, Clausewitz, or Müffling and became the architect of the various victories in the Second Schleswig War (i.e., Danish-German War) in 1864, the Austro-Prussian War (German War) in 1866, and the Franco-Prussian War (Franco-German War) in 1870/71. Moltke's success is based on several factors of success that we have already discussed. We would like to emphasize two more factors again:

Fundamental principles for success according to Moltke	
1	"The education of the subordinate to act independently in the context of the whole war situation,
2	and the art of ordering only that, but also everything, which can be executed with certainty."

Table: Principles of warfare according to Moltke (Möbius and Bigge 2023)

In a nutshell: **Moltke requested and enabled the independence or autonomy of subordinates and focused on the feasibility** (i.e., successful implementation and strategic fit).

"Moltke alone never clung to principles which in themselves might be quite correct, but which did not suit the momentary situation" (Möbius and Bigge 2023, freely translated).

That means: **no dogmatism and no straitjacket in thinking!** General Bigge (one of Moltke's biographers, who met him personally in the 1880s when Bigge was a young General Staff Officer under the command of the already aged General Field Marshal) also highlighted some of Moltke's main character traits:

	Moltke's personal success factors
1	**"Inclination for simplicity"**
2	**"View for the reality of things"**
3	Skillful **recognition of the change of circumstances**
4	**Consideration for the personality** of the sub-leaders
5	**Clear commands** and directives
6	**Modesty** (his nickname was "the Great Silent One")
7	**Velocity and energy**
8	**"Spirit of boldness and determination** that knows only one task: **the offensive, both strategic and tactical"**
9	**Curiosity and sense for sciences, technology** (e.g., the telegraph) **or new solutions** (e.g., the railroad)
10	**Imperturbable calm**
11	**Decisiveness and courage** (to "achieve a great purpose, you have to dare to do something")

Table: Moltke's character traits according to Bigge (Möbius and Bigge 2023)

Moltke drew up detailed plans, adjusting them daily, revising or modifying them (as in the wars of 1866 and 1870/71) or discarding them when conditions changed (as in the Second Schleswig War in 1864), and creating entirely new plans (which followed the original strategy). However, he has been a realist:

"No operational plan extends with any certainty beyond the initial encounter with the main enemy force" (according to Moltke, see Möbius and Bigge 2023, freely translated).

President Eisenhower probably came to the same conclusion: **"Plans are worthless, but planning is everything"**. Back to business: a (corporate) manager is a leader who must fulfill three roles in order to be successful: he or she must be a **personnel developer**, a **corporate developer**, and a **corporate operator** (e.g., in the sense of Collins, Dethmer et al., Drucker or Moltke).

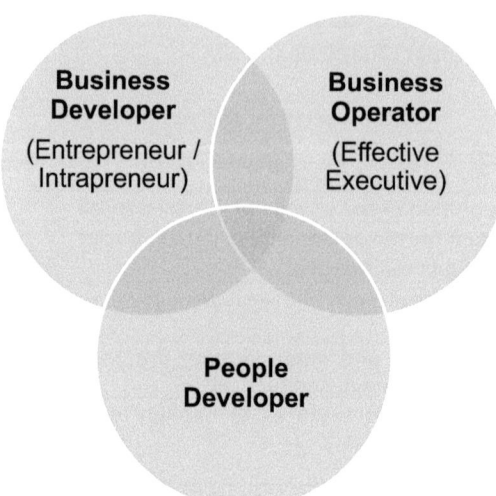

Figure: Being a successful (business) leader; the three roles of a (business) leader

And as we will see in the next chapter: **We should never make false compromises when it comes to people**, see First WHO, then WHAT (Collins 2020). Excellence must be sought at all levels: e.g., the best salespeople, truck drivers, engineers, plant firefighters. A perfect example is provided by Georges Nagelmackers, the "inventor" of the Orient Express with his love of perfection in terms of staff (hiring the best), food, design, entertainment program or service. In general: the creation of a myth (Franzke 1998).

"No company is able to grow its revenue faster in perpetuity than its ability to hire enough suitable people to realize the growth and still become a top company. If revenue growth consistently beats employee growth, you simply will not – or cannot – build a top company" (David Packard's Law, see Collins 2020, freely translated).

The right people (executives, managers and employees) are very important for the success of an organization. In addition, as mentioned earlier (Ritter 2013), there are some key concepts (see next figure) to be successful in business, e.g., **first and foremost securing liquidity** (establish appropriate resources and capabilities such as cash and access to finance, see table below), which is much more important than simple profitability or **effectiveness before efficiency**. Therefore, avoid the risk of overtrading (Neale and McElroy 2004).

Figure: Basic strategy concept (Ritter 2013 und 2020)

In addition, Drucker points out, "the concept of maximizing profits is meaningless … The **purpose of a company** is **to find a customer** … The customer decides what a company is" (Drucker 2014a). Let's take a look at what others recommend. For this purpose, we would like to start with the insights Jim Collins gained when he dealt with the questions of how a good company becomes a top company or how a good company can maintain its position (Collins 2020, Collins and Porras 2004). However, we will talk about the importance of innovation and entrepreneurship in a separate chapter.

	Lessons Learned from "Good to Great"
1	Star managers brought in from outside did not perform well.
2	No correlation between compensation for managerial performance and becoming a top company.
3	No evidence found that top companies spent more time on long-term strategic planning.
4	Good-to-great companies focused not only on what they needed to do to move up to the top, but equally on what they didn't do and what they should stop doing.
5	Technology and technological change played no role at all in the transformation to the top company. Technology can accelerate transformation, but it can't trigger it.
6	Mergers and acquisitions also did not play a role. Two mediocre companies do not become a top company.
7	Good-to-great companies cared little about change management, employee motivation, and goal setting. Under the right conditions, issues like retention, lineup, motivation, or change solved themselves.
8	Good-to-great companies had no name or slogan, no event or program to which they attached their transformation. ... They made a revolutionary leap – but not through a revolutionary process. They weren't in booming industries; they were even in struggling industries.

Table: Insights from "Good to Great" according to Collins (2020), freely translated

In their studies, Collins and his team identified seven management principles that foster success.

	The seven management principles
1	Level 5 leadership
2	First who, then what
3	Confront the brutal facts (comment: see Stockdale paradox)
4	Hedgehog concept – Three overlapping circles
5	Culture of discipline
6	Technology accelerators
7	Flywheel

Table: Management principles from "Good to Great" according to Collins (2020), freely translated

One of Collins' insights: "**Leadership** ambition doesn't start with a vision. It **starts with working with the right people** to analyze the current situation and develop a vision … Motivating people is a waste of time … If you have the right people on board, all you have to do is answer the question of how not to rob them of motivation. Ignoring facts is guaranteed to rob them".

Good-to-great companies (Level-5-Leaders + Management Team)	Comparison company (A genius with 1000 helpers)
Level-5-Leaders	Level-4-Managers
First WHO Get the right people on board. Build a superior leadership team.	**First WHAT** Determination of the route. Development of strategy and tactics.
Then WHAT If the right people are in the right positions, you can think about the right way to the top.	**Then WHO** Hire highly skilled "helpers" to make the vision a reality.

Table: "First WHO, then WHAT" according to Collins (2020), freely translated

This second principle is fundamental to Collins: **First WHO, then WHAT** means that it is more important to have the right people on board first who are more than just highly skilled helpers. From personal experience, we would like to confirm this. A lack of skills can be learned, but a lack of attitude or esprit de corps probably cannot. However, some companies would not even exist without a visionary founder or genius pioneer focusing first on the WHAT.

"When employees have discipline, you don't need hierarchy. When thinking is disciplined, you don't need bureaucracy. When you act with discipline, you don't need excessive controls. Combine a culture of discipline with the ethics of entrepreneurship, and you get the magic formula for excellence" (Collins 2020, freely translated). This sounds a bit like Total Quality Management (TQM) or some other integrated approach.

In summary, for Collins, a culture of discipline (i.e., **disciplined people, disciplined actions**, and **disciplined thinking**) is the recipe for entrepreneurial success. In addition, the third management principle (**"Confront the brutal facts"**, also called the **Stockdale paradox**) is also critical to success.

> "You must maintain unwavering faith that you can and will prevail in the end, regardless of the difficulties, and at the same time, have the discipline to confront the most brutal facts of your current reality, whatever they might be" (**Stockdale paradox** according to Collins 2020, freely translated).

> "... I never doubted that I would get through this. I never doubted I could do it. I've always known that I could do the top things. Never doubted it, I can do it. It's clear, I can manage it" (Udo Lindenberg in his song sung in the film "Lindenberg! Mach dein Ding" song "Niemals dran gezweifelt", freely translated).

Focusing, joining all forces, not doing anything half-heartedly, overcoming challenges, all these points lead us in the same direction as the **"Stockdale paradox"**. Collins proposes yet another successful concept, similar to Gay Hendrik's **Zone of Genius** or the **Papa-Rolf-Benno principle**: the **Hedgehog concept**. In a nutshell:

- **What can we become the best at?** It is not a question of what we WANT to be the best at, but what we CAN become the best at (capacities or competencies may still be lacking). Possibly this is an area in which we have not yet been active. And just as importantly, what can't we become the best at – even if that should be part of our existing core business? Collins goes on to say, "If you can't become the best at your core business, your core business can't be the basis of the Hedgehog concept ... Just because you've done something for years or decades, just because something has become your core business, doesn't mean you can become the best at it". Remember Machiavelli's quote in "The Prince" (see page 28).

- **What drives your economic engine?** This is the area where we can make money over a longer period of time. Remember "Establish profit earning potential of resources and capabilities" (Grant 2002) and the basic strategic concept (Ritter 2013).
- **What are we passionate about?** Collins calls it, "What is our true passion? What ignites our passion?" For him, this is "not the idea behind generating enthusiasm, but doing what enthusiasm is already there for".

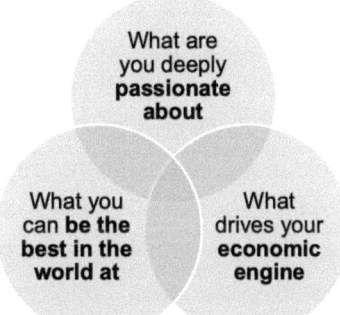

Figure: **Three circles of the Hedgehog Concept** according to Collins (2020). The most important area is the center of this Venn diagram. This is the absolute antithesis of pure denominator management (and wrong downsizing), which Gary Hamel warns against (see Glossary).

Note: Strategy development is a continuous process, see Grant (2002) and Ritter (2013). As entrepreneurs and companies, we have to reinvent ourselves again and again, as Machiavelli already emphasized in "The Prince". This also applies to the Hedgehog concept: formulating the Hedgehog concept is an ongoing process.

The sixth management principle relates to technology: **"technology accelerators"**. We will discuss innovation and entrepreneurship in the next chapter and recommend that you look at the insights of Peter Drucker, Gary Hamel and C. K. Prahalad.

"Good-to-great companies never use technology as a central element to drive transformation. Yet, paradoxically, they are pioneers in their use of carefully selected technologies. **Technology alone**, then, **is not a primary, original cause of rise or fall**" (Collins 2020, freely translated).

One other insight should definitely be emphasized here. Collins recommends that **"stop lists are more important than priority lists"**. This insight is in line with Machiavelli's recommendation to constantly rethink one's strategy and reinvent oneself, or with Hamel and Prahalad, who also recommend a **strategy as forgetting** (learning to forget) instead of a pure, unreflective strategy of learning.

To be transparent with you: Collins' critics insist that his models or explanations are too simplistic and that even the top companies he has identified as such in his studies have sometimes failed dramatically. Furthermore, we should not underestimate the power of a strong vision(ary) like the Wright Brothers. However, since he has studied hundreds of companies, there is definitely some truth in his analyses. And being a top company now does not prevent failure later (as Machiavelli noted). **Our recipes for success must always be adapted when circumstances have changed**. Or better: anticipate it! You have to recognize the changed conditions and then make tough decisions. That's the tricky part. It even sometimes means forgetting what you have learned (see Hamel and Prahalad). We will now conclude this chapter with more insights from "Good to Great" and "Built to Last".

BUILT TO LAST	
Clock Building, not Time Telling	Build an enduringly viable company that can adapt across many generations of leadership and products; the exact opposite of a company designed solely around a single, great leader or business idea.
No Tyranny of the OR **Genius of the AND**	Use your room for maneuver in all directions. Don't choose A or B, but find a way to synthesize A and B – objectives and profit, continuity and change, freedom and responsibility, etc.

BUILT TO LAST	
Cult-Like Cultures **Central ideology**	Embed core values (more essential and enduring principles) and core purpose (raison d'être beyond pure profit) as principles by which you make decisions and keep the workforce excited about your cause over time.
Preserve the Core / Stimulate Progress	Keep the core ideology as the core while promoting change, improvement, innovation and renewal. Change your policies and practices, but stick to your core values and goals. Set risky, Big Hairy Audacious Goals (BHAG) and try to achieve them in alignment with your core ideology.

Table: "Built to Last" according to Collins (2020); see also Collins and Porras (2004)

	Management-principles from "Good to Great"	Connection to the management principles of durable top companies
		Disciplined People
1	**Level 5 leadership**	• **Clock Building, not Time Telling:** Level 5 leaders build companies that work without them, rather than making themselves irreplaceable to boost their own egos. • **No Tyranny of the OR / Genius of the AND:** Personal humility AND professional determination. • **Cult-Like Cultures / Central ideology:** Level 5 leaders are committed to the company and its values and goals; their own success is subordinate to that of the company. • **Preserve the Core / Stimulate Progress:** Level 5 leaders are relentless in driving progress and insist on tangible results – even if it means firing their own brother.
2	**First who, then what**	• **Clock Building, not Time Telling:** Clarifying the WHO-questions first is watchmaking; answering the WHAT-questions (strategy determination) first is just time telling. • **No Tyranny of the OR / Genius of the AND:** Get the right people on board AND get rid of the wrong ones. • **Cult-Like Cultures / Central ideology:** Those who act according to the First-Who-Maxime select their employees primarily according to their conformity with the central corporate values and goals rather than according to their skills and knowledge. • **Preserve the Core / Stimulate Progress:** FIRST WHO means change from inside out that reinforces core corporate values.

	Management-principles from "Good to Great"	Connection to the management principles of durable top companies
	Disciplined Thought	
3	Confront the brutal facts	• **Clock Building, not Time Telling:** Creating a working climate in which you take the facts seriously is clock building, especially if you structurally anchor the possibility to appeal. • **No Tyranny of the OR / Genius of the AND:** Face the harsh reality AND still hold steadfastly to your belief that success is at the end – the Stockdale paradox. • **Cult-Like Cultures / Central ideology:** Facing reality provides clarity on what core values a company really follows and would like to follow. • **Preserve the Core / Stimulate Progress:** A look at the facts makes it clear what needs to be done to promote further development.
4	Hedgehog concept – Three overlapping circles	• **Clock Building, not Time Telling:** The establishment of the "Council" is classic clockmaking art. • **No Tyranny of the OR / Genius of the AND:** Deep understanding AND absolute simplicity. • **Cult-Like Cultures / Central ideology:** The circle "What is your true passion?" overlaps with the central values and the core objectives. Declare only those values as core that you are passionate about and would never, under any circumstances, give up. **Preserve the Core / Stimulate Progress:** Big Hairy Audacious Goals (BHAG) result from insight; bad BHAG result from bragging. Great BHAG fit the intersection of the three circles exactly.
	Disciplined Action	
5	Culture of discipline	• **Clock Building, not Time Telling:** Where only strong personalities provide the necessary discipline, only the time is announced; true clockmaking craftsmanship builds a sustainable culture of discipline. • **No Tyranny of the OR / Genius of the AND:** Freedom AND Responsibility. • **Cult-Like Cultures / Central ideology:** A culture of discipline drives out those who do not share an organization's values and standards. • **Preserve the Core / Stimulate Progress:** In a culture of discipline, people can be given more freedom to experiment.
6	Technology accelerators	• **Clock Building, not Time Telling:** Technology as an acceleration factor is an essential part of the clock.

	Management-principles from "Good to Great"	Connection to the management principles of durable top companies
		• **No Tyranny of the OR / Genius of the AND:** Avoid technical fads AND be a pioneer in the use of new technologies. • **Cult-Like Cultures / Central ideology:** In a top company, technology serves the core company values, not the other way around. • **Preserve the Core / Stimulate Progress:** The right technology accelerates the flywheel and brings the company closer to its BHAG.
	Turn upon turn, building momentum until a point of breakthrough, and beyond	
7	**Flywheel (instead of vicious circle)**	• **Clock Building, not Time Telling:** The flywheel effect ensures sustainable acceleration and does not require a charismatic visionary to motivate employees. • **No Tyranny of the OR / Genius of the AND:** Evolutionary growth AND revolutionary results. • **Cult-Like Cultures / Central ideology:** Vicious circles almost always prevent the anchoring of central values and objectives, although employees constantly ask themselves: "Who are we? What do we want?" • **Preserve the Core / Stimulate Progress:** The steady push of the flywheel and the constant acceleration until the moment of turnaround create perfect conditions for the anchoring of central values and the simultaneous promotion of anchoring and further development.

Table: "Good to Great" and "Built to Last" according to Collins (2020), freely translated. Note: In "Good to Great" Collins forms the link to his earlier work "Built to Last". Collins later came to the realization, perplexing to himself, that his debut work "Built to Last" was actually the sequel to "Good to Great".

In a nutshell: Customer focus (instead of simple profit maximization), reaching the **Zone of Genius**, applying the **Hedgehog concept**, the **Papa-Rolf-Benno principle** and the **Culture of discipline** (having the right people on board) can lead to success. Furthermore, **technology in and of itself is not a "game changer"** according to Collins. However, the business concepts should be based on innovation and entrepreneurship. Let's look at that in the next chapter.

Success Through Innovation and Entrepreneurship

"Innovation creates future" (Professor Hans-Jürgen Warnecke – former president of the Fraunhofer-Gesellschaft).

By and large, there is a consensus that innovation drives success. Of course, this is not necessarily the case with pure inventions. Therefore, please note the difference between a pure invention and a commercially successful innovation. There are three types of innovations (according to Grant, see also Glossary): 1) **innovative products and services**, i.e., product innovations such as the steam engine; 2) **process innovations** such as 3D printing as a new manufacturing process; and 3) **strategic innovations**. These also include new business models, such as Internet-based business models.

"Contrary to the widespread belief in the magic of invention and innovation, 'flashes of inspiration' are exceptionally rare. I don't know of a single one that turned into an innovation. In all the cases I know of, it remained a brilliant idea" (Drucker 2014a, freely translated).

Instead of flashes of inspiration, about 90% of all effective innovations are based on **"careful analysis and systematic and hard work"** according to Drucker.

	The seven sources of innovation opportunity
1	The **unexpected successes** and **failures** of the **organization**, as well as the unexpected successes and failures of its **competitors**
2	**Incongruities**, especially those in the **production** or sales **process**, or contradictions in the **behavior** of customers
3	**Process requirements**
4	**Changes in industry or market structure**
5	**Demographic change**
6	**Changes in importance and perception**
7	**New knowledge**

Table: Commandments for targeted, systematic innovation – "The seven sources of innovation opportunity" according to Drucker (2002), freely translated

In addition to a systematic development approach to innovation (see Glossary and Brown et al. 2002), as also recommended by Grant (2002) or Vahs and Brem (2015), Drucker makes a noteworthy observation. Of course, that sounds a bit provocative:

"First of all, you should not try to be particularly smart. **Innovations must be carried out by normal people**. If they are to have any chance of success, they should be supervised by imbeciles or at least by very limited people. After all, incompetence is the only thing that abounds. **Anything that is overly clever in design or execution is very likely to fail**" (Drucker 2014a, freely translated).

"**Any economic activity is by definition 'risky'. But defending the past – that is, refusing to innovate – is much riskier than shaping the future**. The innovators I know are successful when they manage to identify and contain the risks. They are successful when they succeed in systematically analyzing, precisely defining and exploiting the sources of innovation opportunity. It does not matter whether the opportunity involves a low and clearly defined risk – this applies, for example, to the perception of an unexpected opportunity or the satisfaction of a process requirement – or whether it is an opportunity for a knowledge-based innovation that involves much greater, but still definable, risks. **Successful innovators are conservative, and they have to be. They do not look for risks, but for opportunities**" (Drucker 2014a, freely translated).

Important for successful innovation management is not only a **systematic, structured approach** (see Grant 2002), but also **disciplined action and thinking** (see Collins 2020), as well as appropriate **risk management** (Drucker 2014a), but above all the **successful exploitation of opportunities** (see Drucker 2014a and Collins 2020). Remember **kairos** and **serendipity** stratagem no. 12 (Senger 2016a and 2016b, see also pages 54 and 58)?

"... He stated, 'Your statements astound me. I believe that there is hardly anyone who knows more successful innovators or entrepreneurs than I do. But I have never met an 'entrepreneurial personality'. **However, the successful entrepreneurs I know all have one characteristic – and only this characteristic – in common: They are NOT willing to take risks**. They try to determine the necessary risks and to reduce them as far as possible. If they would not do that, they would not be successful. As for me personally, if I had an inclination to take risks, I would have gone into real estate or commodities trading, or I would have fulfilled my mother's wish to become a painter.' That experience coincides with my experience. ..." (Drucker (2002), quoting a successful businessman and entrepreneur, freely translated).

Interestingly, the average success rate of innovation projects is quite low, see figure below.

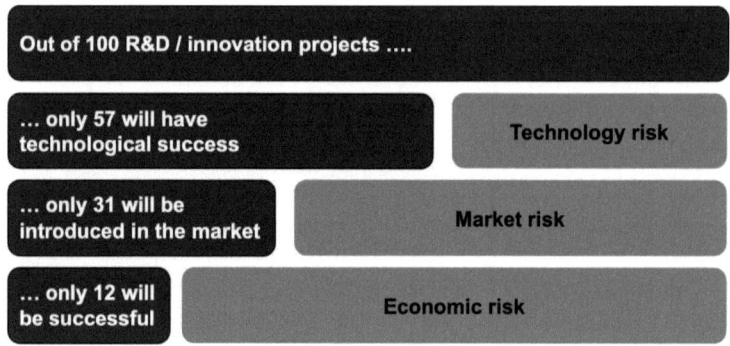

Figure: The success rate of innovation projects according to Vahs and Brem (2015), freely translated. Hint: Robert Grant found out a similar success rate of (only) 10 to 30% with regard to the implementation of (corporate) strategies (Grant 2002).

Technical limits can prevent the feasibility of certain solutions. However, there are often other reasons why "good" technical solutions fail on the market: for example, solutions are developed that are technically feasible but do not meet customer needs or are launched too early or too late on the market. An interesting approach to mitigate the risk of new developments is the development of a so-called **Minimum Viable Product**, as required by agile management, for example (Ritter 2020 and 2021). By involving the customer more closely and delivering a Minimum Viable Product, you meet customer expectations much earlier and much better than with conventional approaches. According to the figure, in contrast to the incremental approach with the Waterfall-based approach, you only deliver a saleable solution at the end.

Waterfall

Incremental / Agile

Figure: A simplistic comparison of Waterfall and incremental (agile) approach

"**An innovation requires the combined energy of a joint effort**. It also depends on the people entrusted with its implementation understanding each other, and this also requires unity. **Diversity and fragmentation threaten this unity**" (Drucker 2014a, freely translated). See Bundling/concentration of all forces (page 99).

Many innovations are based on the **transfer of a solution idea** into a completely new area or are based on knowledge from different areas and collaboration of people with different scientific, technical or cultural backgrounds. It is noteworthy that Drucker warns against dispersal and false diversity. And let us remember Clausewitz: combined efforts (see also page 99). David Pink came to similar conclusions (see Symphony) when he also dealt with questions about success in his book "Why Right-Brainers Will Rule the Future", see his so-called **"Six Senses"**.

"Our brains are divided into two hemispheres. The left hemisphere is sequential, logical, and analytical. The right hemisphere is nonlinear, intuitive, and holistic ... **left brain capabilities that powered the Information Age – are necessary but no longer sufficient**" (Pink 2008).

Not just function but also DESIGN	"It's no longer sufficient to create a product, a service, an experience, or a lifestyle that's merely functional. Today it's economically crucial and personally rewarding to **create something** that is also **beautiful, whimsical, or emotionally engaging**."
Not just argument but also STORY	"When our lives are brimming with information and data, it's not enough to marshal an effective argument. Someone somewhere will inevitably track down a counterpoint to rebut your point. The essence of persuasion, communication, and self-understanding has become the ability also to fashion a **compelling narrative**."
Not just focus but also SYMPHONY	"Much of the Industrial and Information Ages required focus on specialization. But as white-collar work gets routed to Asia and reduced to software, there's a new premium on the opposite aptitude: **putting the pieces together**, or what I (i.e., Daniel Pink) call Symphony. What's in greatest demand today isn't analysis but synthesis – seeing the **big picture** and, crossing boundaries, being able to combine disparate pieces into an arresting new whole."
Not just logic but also EMPATHY	"The capacity for logical thought is one of the things that makes us human. But in a world of ubiquitous information and advanced analytic tools, logic alone won't do. What will distinguish those who thrive will be their ability to understand what makes their fellow woman or man tick, **to forge relationships**, and to care for others."
Not just serious-ness but also PLAY	"Ample evidence points to the enormous health and professional benefits of laughter, lightheartedness, **games and humor**. There is a time to be serious, of course. But too much sobriety can be bad for your career and worse for your general well-being. In the Conceptual Age, in work and in life, we all need to play."
Not just accumu-lation but also MEANING	"We live in a world of breathtaking material plenty. That has freed hundreds of millions of people from day-to-day struggles and liberated us to pursue more significant desires: **purpose, transcendence, and spiritual fulfillment**."

Table: The Six Senses according to Pink (2008)

"Future is something you create, not something that happens to you" (Gary Hamel).

As already mentioned, we can distinguish between product, process and strategic innovations. As Hamel and Prahalad (1997) have shown, business model innovations (i.e., **Business Concept Innovation** = a radical solution as opposed to incremental change) are the most promising. For example, a new software feature (such as printer function) is less significant to customers and users than a new, radical business model (such as Internet commerce when it has been introduced):

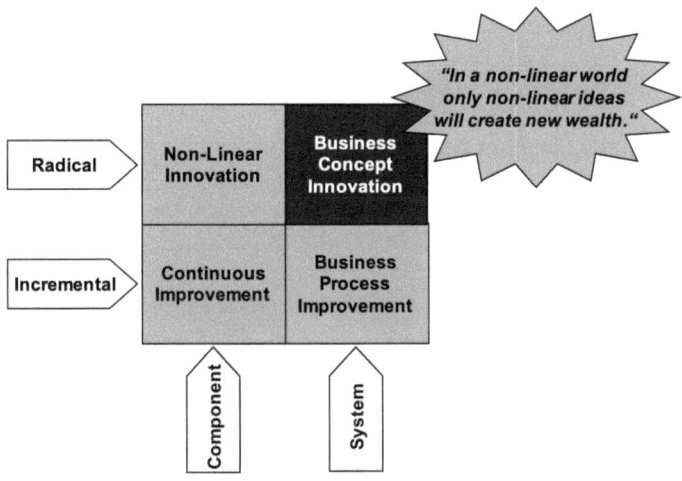

Figure: Business Concept Innovation (Hamel 2002)

Remark: Osterwalder and Pigneur (2011) list a number of business models: e.g., long tail business models, multi-sided platforms, free(mium) or open business models. Hoffmeister (2015) distinguishes between four types of digital business models such as Multilateral / Interactive Business Models, Broadcast, Multi-Agent System and Software-as-a-Service. In **"Competing for the future"**, Gary Hamel and C. K. Prahalad (1997) pose the question of what we should be dealing with in the future as opposed to today.

Today	In 5 ... 10 years
Which clients do you serve TODAY?	Which clients will you serve IN THE FUTURE?
How (by which channels) do you reach clients TODAY?	How (by which channels) will you reach clients IN THE FUTURE?
Who are your competitors TODAY?	Who will be your competitors IN THE FUTURE?
What is the basis of your competitive advantage TODAY?	What will be the basis of your competitive advantage IN THE FUTURE?
What is the basis of your profit/marge TODAY?	What will be the basis of your profit/marge IN THE FUTURE?
What are your competencies or capabilities TODAY?	What will be your competencies or capabilities IN THE FUTURE?

Table: "Competing for the future" according to Hamel and Prahalad (1997). Note: Hamel and Prahalad estimated that top management spends less than 3% of its time planning for the long-term future. Decide for yourself whether this is sufficient.

Interestingly, Drucker calls for innovations to be created for the now.

"Finally, **you should not try to innovate for the future. Innovation should be for the present!**" (Drucker 2014a, freely translated).

At first glance, this seems to be a fundamental contradiction, but it is not necessarily one. Of course, innovations don't come out of nowhere. They have a certain lead time and they **must be introduced at the right time** – not earlier and not later. Furthermore, a successful company must also **earn money today. Cash is the lifeblood of business**. We can win additional insights from Drucker's 1985 work "Innovation and Entrepreneurship".

1	Attack quickly and by all means.
2	Fill the gap left by the competitor (i.e., by doing it better than the innovator).
3	Find and occupy a niche.
4	Strategic innovation: creating new value for the customer.

Table: Strategies of the entrepreneur according to Drucker (2014a), freely translated

For us, one lesson learned is: **Always think like an entrepreneur or intrapreneur**. One organization that embraces this principle is the Fraunhofer-Gesellschaft, for example, where, as a research organization, employees are not only expected to develop application-oriented solutions, but should also always think economically and entrepreneurially. Back to Hamel and Prahalad:

Not only ...	But also ...
The challenge of competition	
Reengineering of processes	Renewal of strategies
Restructuring organization	Change / Transition of industry
Competition for market shares	Battle for opportunity shares
Finding the future	
Strategy as learning	Strategy as forgetting
Strategy as positioning	Strategy as foresight
Strategic plans	Strategic architecture
Mobilization for the future	
Adaptation strategy	Strategic stretch
Strategy as resource allocation	Strategy as resource accumulation and leverage
To reach the future first	
Competition in a given industry structure	Competition to shape the future industrial structure
Competition for product leadership	Competition for leadership in core competencies
Competition as a single entity	Competition as alliance
Maximization the rate of new product "hits"	Maximization of insights into new markets
Rapid market maturity	Quickly outpace the competition worldwide

Table: The new strategy paradigm, see "Competing for the future" according to Hamel and Prahalad (1997), freely translated

Note: **Technology is not synonymous with innovation**. It can be an accelerator (see Collins' comment, see also pages 74, 78, 80 and 81), but it can also have some limitations.

"How is technology going to change business in the future?" ... **"It will accelerate all good and bad trends. ... High tech without high touch does not work**, and the more influential technology becomes, the more important the human factor that controls technology becomes, particularly in developing a cultural commitment to the criteria in the use of that technology" (Covey 2020).

Strategic Success in War and Business

> "Strategy is about winning" (Grant 2002).

> **The best solution to a conflict is to win without having to fight**" (Musashi 2021, freely translated).

When we talk about management and business strategies, we quite often mean competitive strategies in the sense of Michael Porter (differentiation and cost leadership), market- or resource-based, revolutionary and innovative strategies in the sense of Hamel and Prahalad, see Business Concept Innovations, or implementation strategies, imitation avoidance strategies, or timing strategies (waterfall, sprinkler and combined strategies), or strategies for very specific areas such as R&D, logistics, HRM, etc. (Grant 2002, Grichnik et al. 2017, Hamel and Prahalad 1997, Kutschker and Schmid 2011, Porter 1999, Ritter 2013). However, the military element or background of these strategies is almost forgotten. To put it more clearly: management strategies can be very aggressive and decisive for the survival of an organization. They range from coexistence and cooperation to fierce competition and aggressive conflicts such as the "Royal Gorge War" (railroad war of the Rio Grande and Santa Fe involving Bat Masterson and Doc Holliday) and the "Lincoln County War" (cattle war in which "Billy the Kid" became the avenger) or even collusion, i.e., anti-competitive agreements. So, what might we learn from military strategists for ourselves and our organizations? Kotler and Singh, for example, classified military strategies and applied them to business strategies. To better explain this, the marketing expert Jobber presented some examples, see table below (Jobber 2001).

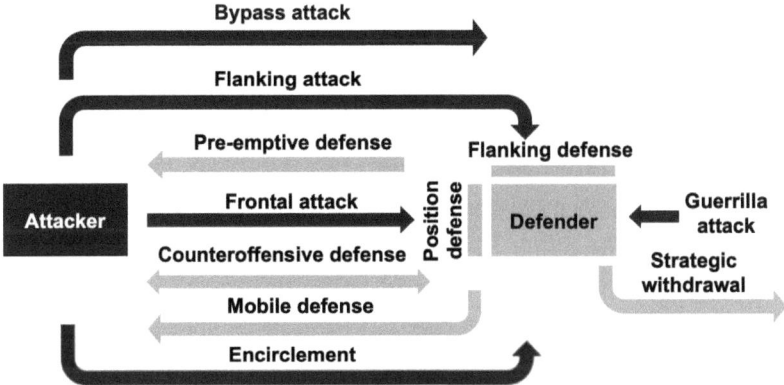

Figure: Attack and defense strategies according to Kotler and Singh (Jobber 2001)

Strategy	The meaning in the business context	(Historic) Examples
Frontal attack	Attack the market leader (e. g., applying cost related strategies; risk of retaliation)	Komatsu versus Caterpillar
Flanking attack	Attack dedicated regions or markets where defender is poorly represented	Unilever versus Mars
Encirclement	Attack all markets or locations at the same time	Mobile phones, cars industry
Bypass attack	Change the rules of the game (e. g., develop new products)	Digital instead of analogue watches
Guerrilla attack	Unpredictable price discounts, sales pro-motion, heavy advertising in a few regions	Local car dealers
Counter-offensive defense	Imitate the attacker (e. g., by heavy price cuttings, hit the attacker's cash cow); encircle attacker (e. g., launch new brands in different price categories)	PC market: Apple launching Macintosh against IBM
Position defense	Build a fortification (e. g., by patents or brand building)	Mobile phone market
Mobile defense	Diversification	Imperial Tobacco (food market)
Flanking defense	Defend unprotected markets	GM launching small cars
Pre-emptive defense	Continuous innovation, R&D, new product development	Pharmaceuticals, chemical industry
Strategic withdrawal	Harvest (and withdraw from markets)	Nokia, GE / Siemens

Table: Attack and defense strategies in the context of business (Jobber 2001)

> **"In peace prepare for war, in war prepare for peace**. The art of war is of vital importance to the state. It is a matter of life and death, a road that leads to safety or to ruin. Therefore, it must not be neglected under any circumstances ..." (Sunzi 2001, freely translated).

"War is the father of all things"; this is a 2.500-year-old, alleged quote from Heraclitus of Ephesus. At about this time, a Chinese scholar and general, Master Sun (Sunzi), studied the subject of strategy and summarized his thoughts in a work still extant today, **"The Art of War"**. This work has not only retained its great importance for military strategies to this day, but is an unparalleled testimony on the subject of strategy. The best way, of course, is to read the entire work. In the following, we will at least briefly underline a few of the highlights.

> "Unhappy is the fate of those who try to win their battles and succeed in their attacks without encouraging daring, for the result is a waste of time and general stagnation. The enlightened ruler works out his plans long beforehand; the good general uses his powers. He rules over his soldiers by his authority, welds them together by loyalty and faith, and makes them serve him by rewards. If faith wanes, disruption will result; if rewards fail, orders will not be heeded" ... "Do not move unless you see an advantage; do not use your troops unless there is something to be gained; do not fight unless the situation is critical. No ruler should send troops into the field just to indulge a whim; no general should start a battle out of anger. Anger may turn to joy in time; anger may be followed by contentment. But a kingdom once destroyed can never be rebuilt; nor can the dead be brought back to life. Thus, the enlightened ruler is prudent and the good general is full of caution. This is the way to keep a country at peace and an army intact" (Sunzi 2001, freely translated).

"The Art of War" is divided into thirteen chapters covering the following topics: 1.) Planning, 2.) On Warfare, 3.) The Sword in the Scabbard, 4.) Tactics, 5.) Energy, 6.) Weak and Strong Points, 7.) Maneuver, 8.) Tactical Variants, 9.) The Army on the March, 10.) Terrain, 11.) The Nine Situations, 12.) Attack by Fire, and 13.) The Use of Spies. Sunzi emphasizes the value of the following virtues for success: **courage, sincerity, wisdom, discipline and rigor; and,**

of course, decisiveness. A recurring element in Sunzi's work is the theme of **espionage and deception** (i.e., applying stratagems). **Speed, the right amount of time** and **the right timing for decisions** are also important success factors.

Topic	Comment / Quotation
Planning	**The general who wins a battle makes many calculations in his mind before the battle**. The general who loses makes hardly any calculations beforehand. Thus, many calculations lead to victory and few calculations lead to defeat – no calculations lead to absolutely nothing! By paying attention to this point, I (i.e., Sunzi) can predict who will win or lose.
Advantage of time versus numerical superiority	While we have heard of foolish haste in war, prudence has never been associated with long delays ... **The advantage of time –** that is, being a little ahead of the enemy – **has often been more important than numerical superiority** or the finest arithmetic games with supplies ... **Your great aim in war should be victory, not a protracted campaign**.
Greatest achievement	Fighting and winning in all your battles is not the greatest achievement. **The greatest achievement is to break the enemy's resistance without a fight**.
Five essential conditions for victory	For there are **five essential conditions for victory:** 1) He will win who knows when to fight and when not to fight. 2) Victory will come to him who knows how to deal with superior and inferior forces. 3) He will be victorious whose army is inspired by the same spirit in all ranks. 4) Victorious will be he who waits well prepared to tackle the unprepared enemy. 5) He will be victorious who is militarily capable and does not have to reckon with the interference of his ruler.
Knowing the enemy and yourself	1) **If you know the enemy and yourself, you need not fear the outcome of a hundred battles.** 2) If you know yourself but not the enemy, you will suffer defeat for every victory you win. 3) If you know neither the enemy nor yourself, you will be defeated in every battle.
The good and wise fighter	1) **Therefore, the good fighter is terrible in the storm and swift in his decision**. ... 2) The wise fighter pays attention to the effect of combined energy and does not ask too much of the individual. He takes individual talents into account and uses each man according to his abilities. **He does not demand perfection from the incapable.**
Five dangerous mistakes	There are **five dangerous mistakes** that any general can make. The first two are: 1) **Recklessness**, which leads to destruction; and 2) **Cowardice**, which leads to being taken prisoner. 3) The next is a **sensitive sense of honor**, which is

Topic	Comment / Quotation
	susceptible to shame; and 4) an **unbridled temper**, which can be provoked by insults. 5) The last of these faults is **excessive concern for the welfare** of the men, which makes the general prone to grief and trouble, for in the end the troops suffer more from the defeat or at best the prolongation of the war which will be the result.
Discipline and punishment	If, in the training of soldiers, every infraction is punished, then the army will be well disciplined; if not, discipline will be poor. **If a general shows his confidence in his men, yet always insists that his orders be obeyed, then both will gain a profit.** The art of giving orders is not to punish too harshly for minor infractions and not to waver in the face of minor doubts. Uncertainty and excessive severity are the surest methods of undermining the self-confidence of an army.
Six ways to invite defeat	There are six ways to invite defeat: 1) **failure to assess the enemy's strength**; 2) **lack of authority**; 3) **inadequate training**; 4) **unwarranted anger**; 5) **failure to maintain discipline**; 6) **failure to use selected men**.
Leading	**Pay careful attention to the well-being of your men, and do not overestimate them.** Concentrate your energy, and use your forces sparingly. Always keep your army on the move, and devise inscrutable plans.
Secrecy	It is the general's **duty to be silent, and thus to provide secrecy**; to be firm and just, and thus to maintain order. He must be able to confuse his officers and men with false reports and deceptions to keep them completely ignorant.
Prevent betrayal	To prevent betrayal, **you should not spread out your plans beforehand.** There should be no rigidity in your rules and plans.

Table: Lessons from the "Art of War" according to Sunzi (2001), freely translated

And surely enough: Every time you read Sunzi's book, you will gain new insights. One remark: It will remain a **challenge to balance the** desire for **secrecy** ("He must be able to confuse his officers and men with false reports and deceptions to keep them completely ignorant") and for **information and involvement of key stakeholders** (see Robert Grant: agreed goals are essential for the success of a strategy). Let's continue with another Asian strategist, the Japanese Kensei ("sword saint") Miyamoto Musashi (1584-1645). His martial art and school have been handed down to the present day, not least thanks to his **"Book of Five Rings"** (i.e., earth, water, fire, wind and emptiness/void) written in the Reigendô cave shortly before his death. Musashi is revered in the Japan – like Sunzi in China.

"If you want to transfer the principles of martial arts to the field of human leadership, you should surround yourself with people of decent character so that you learn to be a good leader to them, to behave with the right kind, to take care of others, to follow the laws and customs of the country for the sake of order, and to be the most dedicated in everything you stand up for. In this way, one will advance and reap personal honor and success. This is the true way of martial arts. For Terao Magonojô – May 12, 1645 Shinmen Musashi" (Musashi 2021). Sounds like First WHO, then WHAT.

1	I do not act against traditional morality.
2	I am not biased in any way.
3	I do not strive for comfort.
4	I do not overestimate myself, but I hold the people in high esteem.
5	I remain free from greed all my life.
6	I never regret what I have done.
7	I never envy others, either because of their good fortune or because of my own misfortune.
8	I am not grieved at being separated from anyone or anything.
9	I do not blame myself or others.
10	I do not dream of falling in love with a woman.
11	I have no likes or dislikes.
12	I do not refuse any accommodation.
13	I do not claim tasty food for myself.
14	I do not collect antique and rare objects.
15	I do not perform purification ceremonies or live abstinently to protect myself from evil.
16	I do not take pleasure in any utensils except swords and other weapons.
17	I will not hang on to my life in the way of righteousness.
18	I do not desire a comfortable retirement home.
19	I respect gods and Buddha, but I do not depend on them.
20	I will give up my life rather than sully my name.
21	My heart and soul will not deviate from the way of the sword for a moment.

Table: Dokkodô ("The Lonely Way" – 21 rules of self-discipline according to Musashi (2021) – given to Terao Magonojô on May 12, 1645, one week before his death, freely translated

Musashi was mainly concerned with the art of swordsmanship. Therefore, not all details from the "Book of Five Rings" are always interesting or relevant to us. In the following we have therefore made a small selection of Musashi's ideas. Here, too, we recommend studying the original or reading Japanese management books in which individual sword fighting techniques have been transferred to management in an abstracted form.

• You should do your work thoroughly. • One should not take anything lightly. • One should set priorities. • One should sense the moods of one's fellow human beings. • One should recognize when something is impossible.

Table: Findings from the "Book of Five Rings" according to Musashi (2021), freely translated

• Have morally sound thoughts. • Practice intensively at all times. • Familiarize yourself with various arts. • Acquire knowledge about crafts. • Think of benefits and harms in everything. • Look at things in the right light. • Make an effort to grasp even the invisible. • Pay attention to the most inconspicuous little things. • Avoid useless activities.

Table: "The Book of Five Rings" – Rules of Martial Arts according to Musashi (2021), freely translated

Note: Some of Musashi's ideas anticipate lean management concepts like Takt Time or waste avoidance ("useless activities"), see Glossary.

Topic	Comment / Quotation
Proper Tact	"Things are fast or slow in relation to the tact of a situation … So, a **proper tact should never be abandoned in favor of high speed**."
Opponent	"No matter how important the opponent is, **you must never think he is superior**. Otherwise, you have already lost the battle."

Topic	Comment / Quotation
Use every weapon	"In the fight for life and death **one should use every weapon, because to die with an unused weapon in the belt would be senseless.**"
Choose your weapons to suit you	"You must **choose your weapons to suit you, and not try to imitate others** in the process."
Change your weapons	**Taking advantage of the element of surprise by constantly changing** (weapons and techniques).
General aspects	**Self-awareness, knowledge of one's own strengths and weaknesses,** as well as precise knowledge of one's environment and fellow human beings. Furthermore, **list sensitivity**, i.e., recognizing stratagems, is extremely important for success.

Table: Lessons from the "Book of Five Rings" according to Musashi (2021), freely translated. Author's comment: The exclusive fixation only on a type of weapon, a fashion theme, on a specific method, a specific solution or a very specific tool – without taking into account the context – is fundamentally wrong.

In addition to Sunzi and Musahi, Niccolò Machiavelli is often quoted in management, to name a European contribution to the topic of strategy. We need to clear up a misunderstanding here:

"Machiavelli is not, as he was misunderstood until the 20th century, a teacher of evil. He is the first analyst of successful political action and, at the same time, of the destructive and ultimately self-destructive effects of unlimited power and rule. We will urgently need him in the future as well" (Horst Günther in the afterword of Machiavelli's "Discorsi", freely translated).

A main factor of success is based – according to Machiavelli (compare Drucker, see pages 66 and 67) – on the **ideology of "virtù"** (i.e., **personal efficiency, prowess, capability**). We can draw a variety of conclusions from Machiavelli's works beyond that (you will find interesting additional ideas in his remarkable books "Il Principe" and "Discorsi"); perhaps at least a few of his insights are worth mentioning:

"For since men almost always walk in well-trodden paths, and their deeds imitate those of others, a man of spirit, even if he is not able to equal those models in everything, nor even to surpass the virtue of those whom he emulates, must nevertheless always walk in the ways of the great and imitate the noblest patterns, so that, even if he does not reach the goal, he may at least act in their spirit" (Machiavelli 2001, freely translated).

"For the reorderer has for enemies all those who are comfortable in the old order, and lukewarm comrades-in-arms in those who hope to gain in the reordering" (Machiavelli 2001, freely translated).

And even if we repeat ourselves, one insight of Machiavelli's is worth repeating several times: **the need to review and rethink our strategy** for success and to **adapt to new circumstances** with foresight:

"For if a man behaves with prudence and patience, and the circumstances of the time are such that his course of action is good, he succeeds in his undertaking; but if the circumstances change, he perishes, because he does not change his course of action. Now man is seldom so wise as to be able to adapt himself to this change, partly because he cannot leave the path which his natural disposition points out to him, partly because one who has always been fortunate in a chosen path cannot convince himself that it would be good to leave it" (Machiavelli in "Il Principe" (i.e., "The Prince"), written in 1513, freely translated).

Besides Machiavelli, Moltke and Sunzi, Carl von Clausewitz (1780-1831), the author of "**Vom Kriege" ("On War")**, is certainly another exceptional man whose fundamental work will remain relevant in the future. In addition to aspects such as the power of chance, which is often completely disregarded by strategic planners, we must always face a reality in which we must make decisions without really knowing all the facts. Forgetting the "Efficient-Market Hypothesis", let's call it, like Clausewitz, the **"Fog of War"**. "On War" is also an extremely readable book, although many aspects require interpretation if they are to be applied to management, business or personal success. Four aspects are of paramount importance for us, which we call 1) **Bundling / concentration of all forces**, 2) **Focus**, 3) **Time advantage** (as well as the right time and the right amount of time), and 4) **Sustainability** (benefit in the long term):

Bundling / concentration of all forces: "To provide all the power that we have with the highest effort. Any moderation shown here is a lag behind the goal. If success itself were quite probable, it is most unwise not to make the highest effort to be sure of it; because this effort can never be detrimental."

Focus: "To concentrate the power as much as possible where the major strikes are to be done, to face disadvantages on other points, in order to be more certain on the main point of success. This achievement reverses all the other disadvantages."

Time advantage: "Unless hesitation gives rise to particularly important benefits, it is important to get to work as soon as possible. By speed, one hundred measures of the enemy are nipped in the bud and public opinion is won first for us ..."

Sustainability: "To utilize the successes we achieve with the highest energy" (Clausewitz 2003, freely translated).

We started this chapter by looking at business strategy from a military perspective. We want to end this chapter with management professor Robert M. Grant (2002), a member of the Design School, who identified the following success factors for a business strategy (which are mainly in line with the above shown principles):

1	Simple long-term goals that are accepted within the organization
2	Profound understanding of the competition and competitors
3	Objective assessment of one's own resources and competencies
4	Strategic fit (i.e., congruence of an organization's resources, capabilities, values, culture, goals and strategies)
5	Effective implementation

Table: Success factors according to Grant (2002)

Let's now take a brief look at Grant's fifth factor: how to properly implement our recipes for success.

"Implementation is the dark side of strategy" (Prof. Herbert Paul).

To be successful, you should avoid typical management failures or strategic failures, see the **"hidden flaws in strategy"** by Roxburgh (2003):

- **Overconfidence:** Confidence and positive thinking are very important to be successful. However, overconfidence ("most of us prefer being precisely wrong rather than vaguely right") is dangerous, e.g., if the conditions on the market have changed completely (or only partially). Perhaps the successful strategy of the past is no longer applicable. Remember what Machiavelli advised in "Il Principe" (see page 28).
- **Mental accounting:** Wrong decisions are made on the basis of a wrong cost-benefit analysis or wrong wishful thinking. And you can always manipulate decisions somewhat (e.g., if you choose different discount rates or make other overly optimistic assumptions about the future cash flows, see the appraisal methods such as the NPV, see also page 61).
- **Status quo bias:** "People would rather leave things as they are. One explanation for the status quo bias is aversion to loss – people are more concerned about the risk of loss than they are excited by the prospect of gain". New opportunities are not recognized or new challenges are tried to be solved with inadequate, inappropriate methods or concepts. It is the opposite of Moltke's attitude (see pages 70 and 71).
- **Anchoring:** "Present the brain with a number and then ask it to make an estimate of something completely unrelated, and it

will anchor its estimate on that first number". You make decisions based on incorrect assumptions (see Genghis Khan date test, see Glossary), e.g., due to wrong assumptions about the development of the markets.

- **Sunk cost effect:** "throwing good money after bad". Sometimes it is necessary to stop an initiative (think of the divestment proposed by the Arnold's Value-Action Pentagon Model, see Glossary), stop uneconomical production, withdraw from a market and stop doing business invest that you will never benefit from. Or stop using old technology (which may have been the success factor of the past). However, the final decision is postponed or delayed. This behavior has various causes: fear of loss of face, ignorance or arrogance, etc. The problem itself is not resolved, and the problem becomes more and more expensive due to the lack of a decision.
- **Herding instinct:** "This desire to conform to the behavior and opinions of others is a fundamental human trait and an accepted principle of psychology". The same mistakes of the industry leader are often imitated without meaning and reason. In addition, nothing is learned from other industries, especially if you tend to see your own industry for something completely different or very special.
- **Misestimating the future hedonic states:** Management often misjudges the future and does not respond appropriately to changes. Reasons can be wrong analysis and wrong setting of priorities.
- **False consensus:** As important as consensus can be in top management, wrong consensus holds enormous potential for conflict. In this case, a certain variety (diversity) can be helpful.

"No operational plan extends with any certainty beyond the initial encounter with the main enemy force" (according to Moltke, see Möbius and Bigge 2023, freely translated); see also pages 70 and 71.

"Plans are worthless, but planning is everything" (President General Dwight D. Eisenhower, see https://quoteinvestigator.com/2017/11/18/planning/; Status: August 2024).

Implementation is the tricky thing: Welcome to reality! In this context, three figures are noteworthy for us:

- **Only 10-30% of the intended strategies are implemented**, as Grant (2002) found out. Keep this in mind and draw the right conclusions.
- **Out of 100 R&D / innovation projects only 12% will be successful** (Vahs and Brem 2015), see also page 84.
- Furthermore, keep in mind that the **average life span of a company is shorter than a human life**, as Brown et al. (2002) pointed out.

Let's assume that these figures are correct. But what can we actually do to avoid serious mistakes and ensure success? First of all, it is not always bad if not all our planned strategies are implemented. Sometimes completely new opportunities arise and we have to **adapt our strategy flexibly and dynamically** in the spirit of Machiavelli. Moltke revised his detailed strategic plans dynamically, taking into account the current situation at any given time during the war campaigns, almost daily, but followed his original basic idea (Möbius and Bigge 2023). Therefore, above all, we must **develop a sensor for kairos and serendipity** (see Senger) in order to remain successful or become even more successful. According to Henry Mintzberg, the strategy later realized in an organization is not only the result of rational planning of strategies, but emergent strategies that were not written down anywhere, but have evolved out of the enterprise. **Serendipity can be a major driver in this process**.

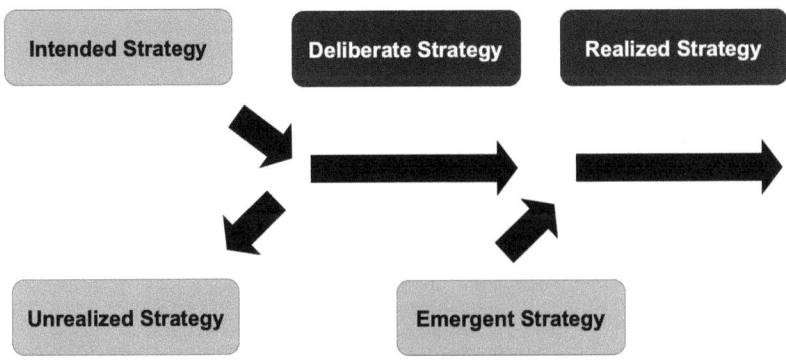

Figure: Mintzberg's Intended and Realized Strategy

***

We've said it before elsewhere: **To be successful, you have to do the right things right**. An integrative, holistic style can be promising. In this context, we have had good experience in developing strategies with our **Strategic Control Loop** (Ritter 2013 and 2020).

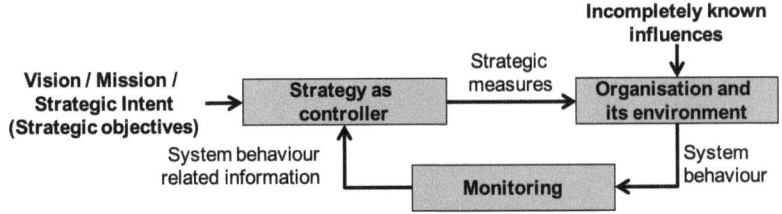

Figure: Strategic Control Loop according to Ritter (2013)

The Strategic Control Loop is also a process model for analyzing and developing strategies in analogy to the analysis and design of dynamic, controlled systems (see also Föllinger 1990).

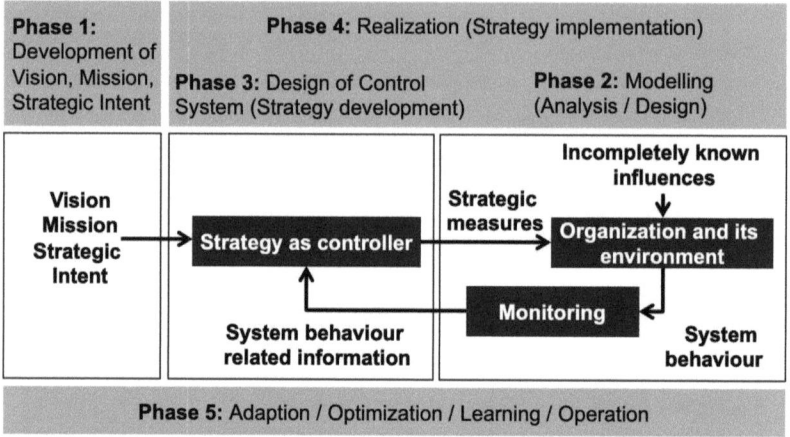

Figure: Strategic Control Loop according to Ritter (2013) – Process model

Our model can also be applied and adapted quite easily for project management. To provide some explanations:

- First of all, the **system to be controlled** is our organization (business).
- **Disturbances/Disruptions** are all internal and external influencing factors such as market disturbances, political crises, etc. And they are mainly unpredictable, partially not causal (we are talking about people) or are only partly under our influence.
- The **controller** is our strategy, which should enable our goals (strategic objectives), derived from our vision, mission and strategic intent. The strategy should not only enable us to follow our vision, but also enable us to react to disturbances/disruptions

in an appropriate manner (and benefit from opportunities/ Kairos/serendipity).

- Our **sensor system** enables us to monitor the relevant controlled process variables. This should be based on meaningful and relevant KPIs (and we should be able to record and calculate them in a simple and unambiguous way without much effort). We must (always) get a clear picture of our current position and the deviation from TO-BE and AS-IS. We must react accordingly!

In a nutshell: we need to develop an adequate strategy (think strategic fit) and adapt it as circumstances change.

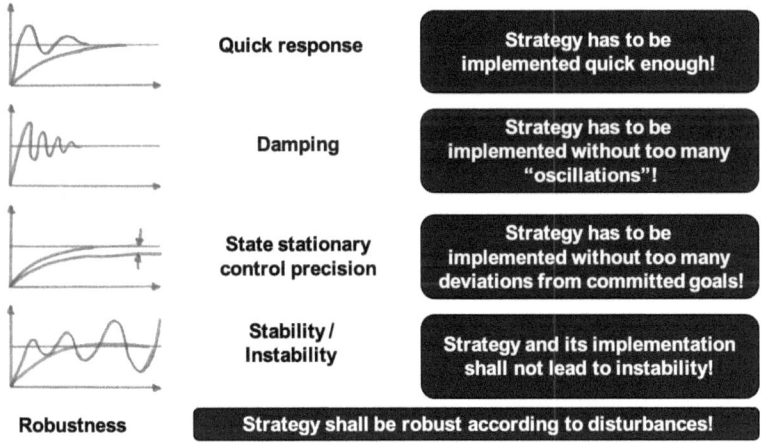

Figure: Control theory in strategy development – requirements according to Ritter: a closed-control loop must be stable, robust, be quick (enough), damped (if necessary, within a range) and precise (within an acceptable range) (Ritter 2020).

A further supporting process model is the **Change Kaleidoscope** (Balogun and Hope Hailey 2004). The Change Kaleidoscope is an interesting framework to analyze and perform changes. The Change

Kaleidoscope and the stakeholder analysis (see Glossary) are our recommendations for change management.

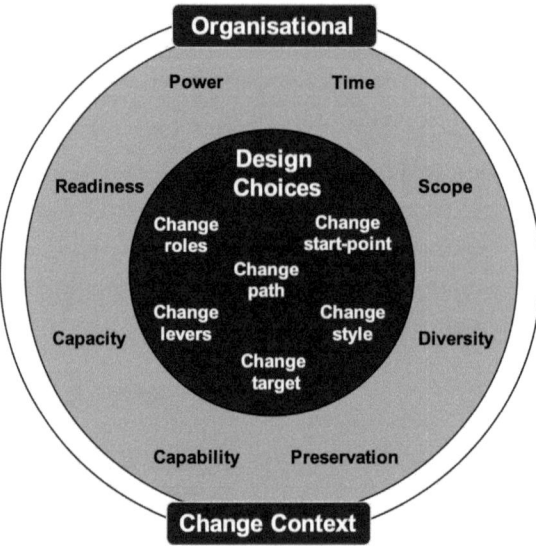

Figure: Change Kaleidoscope (Balogun and Hope Hailey 2004)

You must evaluate the following aspects fairly and also answer the related questions in the context of transformation:

- **Time:** Does the change need to be done quickly? Are we in a crisis? Do we have enough time to act or is the desired change part of long-term, forward-looking strategic planning?
- **Scope:** Does the change affect the entire organization (company, community, state, etc.) or only a part of it? And if so, which one? Is the change a realignment or a complete transformation?
- **Preservation:** Which things, values and achievements should be preserved (not everything is naturally bad) and protected

despite planned or upcoming changes? What is it particularly worth to be preserved? What can or should we give up?

- **Diversity:** Are the individual groups homogeneous or different in their values, norms and attitudes? How different are they (in terms of gender, nationality, age, education and training, etc.)? What are the expected effects?
- **Capability:** How great are our management skills as well as the organizational and individual skills to implement the change in the organization? What skills are needed at all and should they be developed or acquired if necessary? What form of consulting do we need?
- **Capacity:** How many resources (e.g., time, money, tools, manpower) are available for the change process? How many can we afford? Which/what are/is still needed?
- **Readiness for change:** How willing is the organization to change? How strong is the awareness of the need for the planned change? How strong is the motivation to support? What kind of resistance can be expected? What arrangements can we make?
- **Power (i.e., power relationships):** How is power distributed within the organization? How much space do we have?

Decisive for success is not only the correct analysis according to the above questions, but also the corresponding answers and concepts to be developed. There are a few other decisions that need to be made:

- The so-called **change path** describes the type and the result of the considered and planned change. Defining the change path is the first and most important decision in the change process. Basically, we can distinguish four types of changes according to their radicalness **(incremental change or big bang)** and depending on the intended result **(transformation or alignment)**.

- The **change start-point** refers to the area of the organization in which the change was initiated or from which it is controlled. For example, a change can be managed in a top-down style, but it could also be initiated by individuals, even bottom-up (e.g., within "empowered" organizations) or once in individual departments or divisions as so-called "pilots" (i.e., pilot projects). Especially in crisis situations, changes are often initiated in a **top-down style**. Also note the following: The **bottom-up approach** can be quite unpredictable. Especially in empowered organizations with democratic basic processes, decisions are more open-ended and very dynamic (and take longer). This can also be exactly what you want.

- The **change style** describes how the implementation of the change is controlled. The change style can range from coercion to direction, participation, collaboration, education, and delegation. Of course, the change style can have a decisive influence on the acceptance of a change initiative.

- The **change target** describes the **strategic goal**, e.g., also change of values.

- The **change levers** describe the levers and intervention options in the change process that are available to you.

- The change can only be implemented successfully if someone feels responsible for the change process. Different **change roles** are therefore important: leadership, external moderation, e.g., by external consultants, "change action teams" or delegations, e.g., to certain departments (functional delegation). A combination of different change roles very often makes sense (e.g., leadership, change action teams and external consultants).

And as we mentioned above, **clear and committed goals are mandatory for success** (Grant 2002). A word about goals. If you like business novels, we can recommend you Eliyahu M. Goldratt's book, **"The Goal"**. It represents one of the first and – for us – also best business novels due to relevance to industrial operations. It basically follows the method of discourse and dialogue – some would call it the Socratic method. In the novel, the hero of the story, Alex Rogo, is faced with the challenge of becoming a plant manager and dealing with his production problems, which are not his fault but "inherited", securing his location from an impending plant closure, and also solving his marital and family problems. He is helped in this task not only by his team members, but also by his mentor Jonah, who above all repeatedly **points him in the right direction by asking essential questions**. Even if the book is more interesting for people who work in the field of manufacturing and operations and deal with topics such as inventories, bottlenecks, lot sizes, cycle time, throughput, operating costs, levelling (Heijunka) – Goldratt does not explicitly deal with the Toyota Production System in his book – other interested people can also learn from the efficiency and effectiveness problems in a technical operation, even if the result described in the book is then consequently a Manufacturing Execution System. The basic questions, discussions and solution ideas can be profitably transferred to many other areas. One statement should be highlighted: "A factory in which everyone is working all the time is working very inefficiently". Or also: "A system with only single optima is anything but an optimal overall system: in fact, it is a very inefficient system". A lesson can be learned from this and transferred to other areas: **We need free spaces (e.g., time or physical**

resources) and contingency plans (see TUDAPOL principle, see below). The **TUDAPOL principle** is our holistic principle for innovation, development and operation (Ritter 2020).

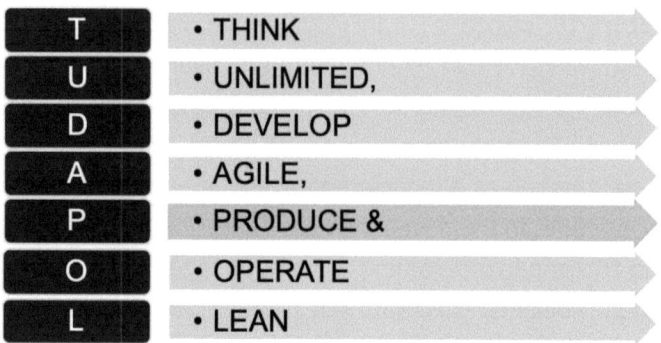

T	• THINK
U	• UNLIMITED,
D	• DEVELOP
A	• AGILE,
P	• PRODUCE &
O	• OPERATE
L	• LEAN

Figure: The TUDAPOL principle according to Ritter (2020 & 2022)

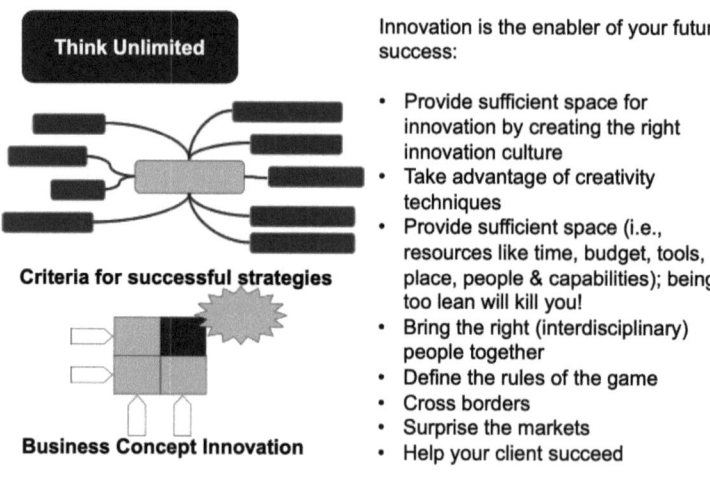

Think Unlimited

Criteria for successful strategies

Business Concept Innovation

Innovation is the enabler of your future success:

- Provide sufficient space for innovation by creating the right innovation culture
- Take advantage of creativity techniques
- Provide sufficient space (i.e., resources like time, budget, tools, place, people & capabilities); being too lean will kill you!
- Bring the right (interdisciplinary) people together
- Define the rules of the game
- Cross borders
- Surprise the markets
- Help your client succeed

Figure: The TUDAPOL principle according to Ritter (2019 & 2020 & 2021)

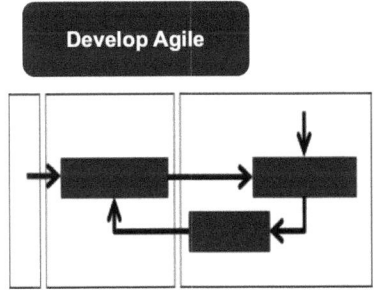

**Frameworks like
Strategic Control
Loop**

Waterfall or classic project management are not bad, but have some limitations. Take advantage of agility:

- Deliver fast and early (time advantage)
- Provide an early working product (increment); that is better than a perfect, but too late delivered solution
- Focus on the things creating value
- Accept that requirements could change
- Take advantage of integrated teams (e.g., DevOps) and early integration
- Think as a control loop
- Agility is to some extend the opposite of being lean: provide space & redundancy & buffer

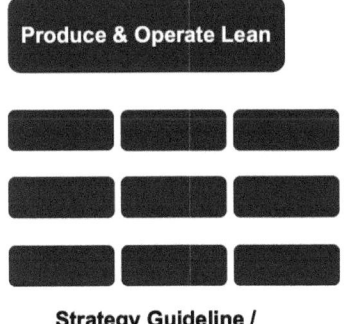

**Strategy Guideline /
Framework**

Focus on value creation as proposed by lean approaches, e.g., by avoiding waste:

- Focus on value creation
- Avoid unnecessary waste
- Reduce complexity
- However: maintain the complexity, flexibility and redundancy you still need. A skeleton is not a living organism!
- Furthermore: enable transformation and sustainability

Figure: The TUDAPOL principle according to Ritter (2019 & 2020 & 2021)

We would like to make a few additions at this point:

TU	**Think Un-limited**	<ul><li>Don't forget the (nine) success factors (page 14)! Identify the pains and gains and don't miss the opportunities and chances; don't forget Arnold's Value-Action Pentagon Model; furthermore, develop appropriate business models (e.g., Long Tail Business Models, Multi-sided platforms, Free (mium), Open Business Models, etc.) and create real Business Concept Innovation and reinvent the game.</li><li>Avoid any straitjackets in thinking and see the limits of models, approaches, methodologies and strategies. Don't be (too) dogmatic. Apply Design Thinking or Lateral Thinking; leave the familiar path (if necessary); use your imagination and your creative potential and follow the Design and Process School; it is not an either-or. Be a Right- AND Left-Brainer; be both at the same time: "No Tyranny of the OR / Genius of the AND!"</li><li>Meeting today's needs is not enough; think about the future! The future may not be an extension of today's world. The future is partially or mostly unpredictable. There will be disruptions, new opportunities and lucky circumstances as well. Continuous improvement is not always enough; sometimes only radical change will help you survive.</li><li>Learn from the past, but forget the past when it becomes a burden; keep the good old concepts and understand the core concepts behind them. Keep or develop an open mind; again, don't be too dogmatic; you can't know every-thing; there is a whole lot to learn.</li><li>Become a conscious leader.</li><li>Let us have fun. It is essential and often forgotten.</li></ul>
DA	**Develop Agile**	<ul><li>Take advantage of Minimum Viable Products.</li><li>Focus on the value proposition and deliver early.</li><li>It is a people business; develop strong relationships.</li><li>Understand and apply agile values (e.g., openness, com-mitment, courage, respect, or focus).</li></ul>
POL	**Produce and Operate Lean**	<ul><li>Take advantage of lean management (concepts), see Toyota Production System. Avoid waste; focus on value streams. However, we need free space (and contingency plans)!</li><li>Increase efficiency and effectiveness (including your communications).</li><li>Reduce complexity (e.g., through decoupling or harmoni-zation).</li><li>Take advantage of knowledge management.</li><li>Take advantage of digitalization.</li></ul>

Table: The TUDAPOL principle in short, see also Ritter (2019, 2020, 2021 and 2022)

We always need some buffer, margin and overcapacity. "Strategic stretch" is good. But we need breathing room and the space to think and act properly. Beyond that, think about serendipity or emergent strategies. From our point of view, what we could transfer and learn in a generalized form from manufacturing to other areas such as IT would be the five focusing steps of **Goldratt's bottleneck theory**, as they can be found in "The Goal":

Step 1	Identify the system's constraints.
Step 2	Decide how to exploit the system's constraints.
Step 3	Subordinate everything else to the above decision.
Step 4	Elevate the system's constraints.
Step 5	If in the previous steps a constraint has been broken, go back to step 1.

Table: The five focusing steps according to Goldratt, see also Theory of constraint; https://en.wikipedia.org/wiki/Theory_of_constraints (Status: August 2024).

In addition to the Change Kaleidoscope and the Strategic Control Loop, we recommend the **Business Model Canvas** (according to Osterwalder and Pigneur) for the analysis, development and implementation of a business model.

Figure: Business Model Canvas (Osterwalder and Pigneur 2011)

We would like to add a supplement from "Good to Great" on the subject of transformation and implementation. Collins talks about the "Flywheel" (upswing) and "Vicious circle" (downswing). In doing so, he and his team have identified a number of indicators to help us determine if we are on the right track. The individual alarm signals should prompt us to take immediate action.

The flywheel effect	The vicious circle
Forward action in harmony with the Hedgehog concept	Disappointing results
Accumulation of visible results	Ill-considered reaction
Employees stick together, energized by results	New course, new strategy, new CEO, new fashion or takeover of another company
Intensifying impetus; the wheel gains momentum	No impetus; the wheel loses momentum

Table: "Flywheel and vicious circle" according to Collins (2020), freely translated

"How to know if you're creating momentum or stuck in a vicious circle"	
Hints that you drive the flywheel (good-to-great company)	Indications that you are stuck in a vicious circle (comparison companies)
You follow the model of boost and turnaround.	You skip the start-up phase and go straight for the breakthrough.
Step by step, turn by turn, you approach the turnaround. You have the feeling of being part of a revolutionary, organic process.	You launch major programs, instigate radical changes, dramatic revolutions and chronic restructurings – always in search of a miracle or savior.
You look the facts unsparingly in the eye to be able to decide with certainty what needs to be done to create new momentum.	You get excited about fads and make all kinds of fuss about your great management instead of going with the facts.
With the help of a clear Hedgehog concept, you ensure coherence and always stay exactly within the three circles.	You display chronic incoherence, waver back and forth, and digress far from the three circles.
You follow the pattern "disciplined people (first who, then what), disciplined thinking, disciplined action".	You get started right away, forego disciplined thinking and don't bother to get the right people on board first.

"How to know if you're creating momentum or stuck in a vicious circle"	
Hints that you drive the flywheel (good-to-great company)	**Indications that you are stuck in a vicious circle (comparison companies)**
You use technology as an accelerator for your Hedgehog concept.	In the face of technological innovations, you run around like a headless chicken because you are afraid of being left behind.
You approach major company acquisitions (if any) after your breakthrough to provide additional momentum.	In a hopeless frenzy of action, you buy up other companies before you have achieved a breakthrough because you hope it will give you the boost you need.
You hardly waste energy on motivating your employees – the contagious drive of your flywheel already takes care of that.	You waste a lot of energy on motivating your people and getting them on track by constantly swearing them to new visions.
You let the results speak for themselves.	You sell future as a substitute for presentable results.
You ensure sustainable consistency; each generation continues the work of its predecessor; the flywheel continuously gains momentum.	You demonstrate sustained inconsistency; each new company boss brings a radical change of course; the flywheel comes to a halt and the vicious circle starts all over again.

Table: "Flywheel and vicious circle" according to Collins (2020), freely translated

For this book, we conducted another set of interviews and did some brainstorming and analysis to gather empirical rules or additional success factors which have been important to us in the past. The order of these "rules" (i.e., a kind of **personal best practice**) is arbitrary and does not represent a valuation.

	Rule	Comment
1	**Papa-Rolf-Benno Principle**	See also Hedgehog concept: "Focus on the things that really interest you, that is your passion, that you can be really good at, and that have great potential for the future – both economically and personally. And don't forget the fun part". Our father/grandfather Rolf came to this realization. As a professor of mechanical engineering, he naturally dealt with the subject of success from different perspectives as well.

	Rule	Comment
2	**Life is a battle, so fight**	Motto of our mother/grandmother. This motto probably goes back to Voltaire: "Ma vie est un combat". Source: https://beruhmte-zitate.de/zitate/125817-voltaire-mein-leben-ist-ein-kampf/. Perhaps less martially phrased: "Giving up is not an option" or "Falling down is not a disgrace, but staying down is". And there's Gay Hendrick's conciliatory suggestion to work on our "Upper Limit Problem". We grow with our tasks.
3	**Going the Extra-Mile**	"Going the extra mile" is not just a consulting phrase. Success is based on a high level of commitment and discipline. That's why we are convinced that a nine-to-five mentality is not enough. That brings us back to Strategic stretch, Resource leverage (Hamel and Prahalad), see also Glossary, and a Culture of discipline (Collins), see also pages 69, 75 and 80.
4	**If you stop getting better, you've stopped being good**	My (Arno) personal motto (probably John Andrewes in 1615): I take it to mean more than just continuous improvement (kaizen). We must never rest on our laurels. We must also remain adaptable and flexible (see Machiavelli, see also page 28) and be open to reinventing ourselves, learning and, above all, maintaining a constant sense of curiosity.
5	**We never leave one behind**	Implicit leadership motto (responsibility and protection): whether in the military or in a professional environment; we have a social obligation to our employees and fellow human beings; see also Conscious Leadership (see also pages 63-65). And that obligates: "Wie Pech und Schwefel!" / "Like pitch and brimstone!" (motto of former German Army Parachute Battalion 261).
6	**Klaus Killmann Rule: "Tun" (Just-Do-It)**	One of the shortest implementation or success rules that our workshop leader at the time expressed in relation to the difficulties of doctoral students who experienced a blockage, seemed to lose their motivation or were even in danger of failing. "Doing", that is, solving problems (pain) and seizing opportunities (gain). Klaus Killmann will always remain gratefully in my (Arno's) memory for his many, very good and feasible ideas; simply a master of his trade. See also: "No longer discuss the nature of the good man, but be such a man" (Marcus Aurelius in his Self-Reflections – Tenth Book, 16).
7	**Jörg Rule: "Better an early, improvement-worthy version than a too-late, perfect version"**	Long before we first heard of the "Minimum Viable Product", Jörg (now a professor of electrical engineering) put it in a nutshell: speed, right balance and right timing are always better than a "perfect" version of a product (such as a promotional publication), but delivered too late (and then can you still call it perfect at all?). Judge for yourself whether a work (or product) created in nine years is really better than one written or developed in "only" four or six years. We must

	Rule	Comment
		never miss the right moment, which brings us back to the topic of kairos.
8	**Alex Rule: "At some point even your favorite topic will piss you off"**	Gay Hendricks is right, of course, that it's great to do work that doesn't feel like work to us – that is, to be in our Zone of Genius. Jim Collins talks about the Hedgehog concept. Of course, Collins is also right with his model of the flywheel, i.e., consistency, related to success. We have to "keep at it". However, I (Arno) agree with the current professor of food technology that there are certainly performing phases, but also phases in which not everything comes so easily to us. So, let's face the brutal facts (see Stockdale paradox, see page 76) and "fight" on and keep our course.
9	**Thinking in terms of a (strategic) control loop**	This is my (Arno) very personal motto – and not only since I had dealt with control engineering as a specialization in my studies. We have to think holistically. We have to constantly record the AS-IS status and permanently keep an eye on our goals. We must recognize deviations from the TO-BE state and the AS-IS state in time ("in real time") and react to them quickly in the sense of our goals, i.e., in the sense of a closed-loop control system (in contrast to an open-loop control).
10	**No dogmatics (remember Moltke and Musashi)**	Musashi (see pages 94-97) is absolutely right when he recommends changing methods (fighting techniques) and tools (weapons) depending on the situation, which then comes as a complete surprise to our "opponents". In our opinion, the fixation on only one method bears a risk. A pianist must of course master his instrument perfectly; managers, engineers, generals or entrepreneurs, on the other hand, must remain mentally flexible. Methods can therefore be helpful in principle, but should never become a straitjacket in thinking.
11	**Papa Daniel Rule: "Serenity"**	"Don't force a solution for a problem today, which you won't and can't solve today anyway or alone. Regenerate and take care of the solution promptly (e.g., the next day). Pay attention to enough sleep and your health. If you sleep over a matter, a problem sometimes looks completely different when viewed in a new light. Moreover, you can now ask for appropriate help that may not have been available to you yesterday, or entrust the right people with solving the problem". As a former captain and member of the board of directors of a large oil company, our father-in-law/grandfather knew and lived through a variety of crises and challenges. Asian composure and Christian-based thinking helped him through.
12	**Helping clients succeed**	Win/Win – in the sense of Stephen Covey (see page 41) – and even better, the focus on THE customer – see Mahan Khalsa (see pages 59-61) – are an important key to success for service providers (such as consultants or development

117

	Rule	Comment
		partners). We must not forget that our view is not necessarily the same as our customer's view. We must learn to understand them and make them successful.
13	Michael Rule	Michael has emphasized one theme again and again for many years: "What do I burn for?" (What is our passion?). This coincides very well with the Hedgehog concept or the Papa-Rolf-Benno principle, but also the Klaus Killmann Rule.
14	Implementation is the dark side of strategy	This is an important insight as formulated by MBA professor Herbert Paul. In addition, Robert Grant sees the adequate implementation of a strategy as one of the key success factors (see page 99 and also "Commitment" and agile values). In short: "Doing the right things right". I (Arno) also recommend thinking outside the box (looking beyond), see BANWAD WAY (Glossary).
15	Never take counsel of your fears	"Never take counsel of your fears" or "Fear is a bad counsellor" (General Thomas Jonathan Jackson, called "Stonewall Jackson"). A universally valid rule – for every area of life. https://beruhmte-zitate.de/zitate/131170-andrew-jackson-angst-ist-ein-schlechter-ratgeber/.
16	Keep moving	It is not only infantrymen who can benefit from a change of position in combat. Stephen Covey accordingly calls it "Being Pro-active" (see page 41). For the most part, this is better than mere reactivity and, above all, self-inflicted passivity. We must remain agile and flexible, i.e., also capable of change and open-minded. Instability is not meant here, of course (see page 105).
17	The Sausack Theory	Our friend Erhan learned this rule from an older Austrian colleague. For him, everyone is a "sausack" (i.e., press head; a kind of bully or idiot is meant) until he or she proves otherwise. For us, this appears to be the shortest formula for protection against the "36 stratagems" and "perfidious opportunists" (see also pages 50 and 52-58).
18	The critical path or the red thread	"Begin with the end in mind" demands Covey (see page 41). We share this view. We therefore recommend recognizing the "red thread" and always paying attention to the "critical path". In other words, we must not only think tactically, but strategically, on the basis of analytical and structured thinking, identify dependencies, anticipate and mitigate problems! For us one of the most important points. Once again: think like a Strategic Control Loop (see pages 103-105)!
19	Roderick Rule: Volatility-Contingency	Create free spaces and contingency plans by applying success factors to compensate for obstacles and unexpected setbacks; balance volatility (see also the TUDAPOL principle).

	Rule	Comment
20	**Roderick Rule: Integrative approach**	Develop social skills (including list-sensitivity, networking, positive communication) + Positive thinking (including sensor for kairos, motivation, physical and mental health) + Risk management (including regular validation of own goals).

Table: Personal best practice success rules

"Klotzen, nicht kleckern!" (Could be translated as "Kick, don't spatter them!", which means: think big, concentrate, do nothing half-heartedly; i.e., the motto of Colonel General Heinz Guderian). See also Clausewitz and page 99.

All the success strategies and recipes for success discussed so far in the previous chapters ultimately have something to do with implementation. In fact, they are (almost) useless if they are not implemented and applied correctly. Let us therefore once again recall what the gurus might think and recommend on the subject of implementation (see previous chapters): Hendricks would advise: Work on your "Upper Limit Problem"; Jim Collins would not only have to refer to his "seven management principles" (see "Good to Great" and "Built to Last") and Peter Drucker, on the other hand, could refer to his own work, e.g., how to be an "Effective Executive – Eight (or Nine) Virtues of Being a Leader". And they would be right. We have already talked about many success factors, which of course cannot be considered in isolation from implementation strategies. Every good principle has to be implemented correctly and consistently, taking into account the specific boundary conditions. For us, it kind of goes without saying that all the points and success factors we have already discussed are somehow ultimately relevant for the implementation: Be it the question of WHAT, be it the question of HOW or further on WHERE TO. This remains a challenge.

Colonel von Blumenthal to General von Moltke in a letter during the Second Schleswig War (1864): "There are probably only a few people who are able to execute a simple thought so easily" (Möbius and Bigge 2023, freely translated).

Success Factors in Business and Management

"Be better than the GAP" (Ryan Gosling aka Jakob Palmer to Steve Carell aka Cal Weaver in the film comedy "Crazy, Stupid, Love.").

We have talked about success in a wide variety of areas. We now want to summarize the most important factors (see previous chapters). In doing so, let's start with the most important individual success factors. You will recognize a number of the factors that we had already discussed and identified: **disciplined action, commitment, effective leadership and strategic thinking**. Strategic thinking and strategic success are based on factors such as **focus, strategic fit** and **effective implementation**.

Individual and strategic success factors		
Individual success factors		
A	**Intelligence & Character**	• Great talent, aptitude and strength of character • Focus on own strengths (not weaknesses) • High chance utilization • (Ability to) inspire others
B	**Ambition**	• (Great) ambition or (strong) will to win and (great) confidence in winning • Never or not being satisfied with unambitious goals (see also BHAG)
C	**Commitment / Engagement**	• (Extreme) diligence and (high) commitment • (Great) willingness to go the extra mile, coupled with a fighting spirit
D	**Discipline**	• Great self-discipline and consistency • Do not give up and do not let setbacks deter you from your chosen course (this does not mean stubbornness, of course)
E	**Efficiency & Effectiveness**	• Achieve more than others in the same time (be the master of your time) • Deliver better quality than others in the same time • Good communication, negotiation and networking skills • Ability to learn from failure

	Individual success factors	
		• High opportunity exploitation and sense of opportunity (serendipity) • If possible, leave nothing to chance • Focus on feasibility • Master complexity
F	**Strategic thinking**	• Be goal-oriented (but flexible) • Long-term, analytical thinking in several steps • Clear, long-term goals • Develop your own ideas (and visions) • Be an entrepreneur
G	**Curiosity & Interest**	• Diverse and/or pronounced interest or curiosity • Lifelong learning • Be an innovator
H	**Courage & Self-confidence**	• Courage to make decisions / decisiveness • Courage to implement and (consistently) pursue decisions / enforce decisions • Self-reflected self-confidence in one's own abilities • Master the Upper Limit Problem (not sabotaging yourself and not letting fear win)
I	**Fortune**	• Lucky circumstances and coincidences • Satisfaction, joy and positive thinking

	Strategic success factors	
J	**Focus**	• Define the right scope • Follow/set the real priorities • Avoid multi-front wars
K	**Time advantage**	• Be faster than the competition ("the enemy") and shorten time-to-market • Speed is often more important than other resource-based advantages • Think Minimum Viable Product. Deliver early, but don't wait for the "perfect" solution • Take the right amount of time and the right point of time
L	**Bundling / concentration of all forces**	• "Strategic stretch" (overstressing, over-stretching organization, resources, capabilities, capacities, etc. to achieve ambitious goals – "going the extra mile"); see also ambitious goals (BHAG) • "Strategic stretch" won't work forever; but never do things half-heartedly

		Strategic success factors
		• Do the things effectively with maximum force and don't lose a "battle" by not using your resources effectively and efficiently
M	Sustainability	• Benefit from a victory. It is not enough to win a "battle" or "war". Secure the future • Strategy development, implementation and improvement is an ongoing activity that never ends • Build the capability/capacity to learn • Create the capability to innovate • Reduce (unnecessary) costs • Create the capability to enable and improve quality and service • Establish the capability for change, for flexibility and transformability • Establish appropriate resources and capabilities and establish profit earning potential of resources and capabilities • Ensure the avoidance of imitation (to be imitated and to imitate the wrong) • Enable easy application of your strategy
N	Simple, agreed long-term goals	• Define clear targets/goals • Communicate them, make relevant stakeholders aware about them • Get and gain their commitment • Develop real (conscious) leadership on your side
O	Profound understanding of competition and competitors	• Understand the context (i.e., opportunities, threats, trends, complementors, etc.) • Prepare to change your mindset (if necessary) to fill the gap • Define the game (if feasible)
P	Objective appraisal of own resources and competencies	• Know your strengths and weaknesses • Analyze the readiness of your people, organization or resources to change and to act appropriately. Are you ready for the change, the new strategy and new culture? • Identify the gaps (and close them or make them obsolete/irrelevant) • Identify where and what you need to build (or leave) and what you need to improve
Q	Consistency (Strategic Fit)	• Align your strategy (and leadership style) with your corporate culture • Get your organization ready for the intended changes and strategy

Strategic success factors		
		• Make sure your strategy, methodology, resources, way of working and corporate culture fit together • Find the right balance and empower your organization in the context of the planned changes (e.g., agile management does not work if teams are not given the required decision-making authority or if there are still too many interfaces)
R	**Effective implementa-tion**	• Don't forget the dark side: the implementation • Avoid implementation failures (see pages 100-101) • Develop and work on becoming a true (conscious) leader • Develop and empower the (right) people • Enforce Leading by mission / Management by objectives, independence of sub-leaders and focus on feasibility • Choose the right change strategy and the right change approach, e.g., Change Kaleidoscope • Think like a "Strategic Control Loop" • Establish the skill and the sustainable ability for change capability (transformability)

Table: Individual and strategic success factors

Success should always be measured by the degree to which we achieve defined goals. And we should also not forget one comforting realization when we try to answer the question of whether we are really successful (as already mentioned in the Preface):

"When it's all said and done, what do we measure ourselves by? If Lansky taught me one thing, it's that there's only one measure in this world that really matters: We measure ourselves by the eyes of those we love" (Sam Worthington aka David Stone on gangster Meyer Lansky, the so-called "Mob's Accountant" played by Harvey Keitel in the 2021 film "Lansky" by Eytan Rockaway).

And there is a little trick that we can learn from agile management to make us feel like winners even if we do not fully achieve the goals, we have set for ourselves: the definition of so-called "stretch objectives" (i.e., additional, optional (not committed) goals). It is often in the nature of things that ambitious goals cannot always be fully achieved in time. Consequently, if we took these "committed" goals as a basis for evaluating our success, we would rarely achieve 100% and never be completely satisfied. But Mintzberg already pointed out that the strategy realized in the end is the sum of "Emergent Strategies" and "Intended Strategies" minus the strategies not realized (see page 103). By analogy, our results are the sum of the committed and stretch objectives we have achieved. For example, if we achieved only 90% of our committed goals, but additional goals beyond that "on top", which we defined as "stretch objectives", so to speak, whose value we assessed as 20%, we would have even achieved 110% in the end; that feels a lot better than just 90%. To be fair, it must be said that this is not a purely psychological trick or "creative accounting", but rather a legitimate approach, since we usually really do significantly more and also achieve something different than what was once originally planned. It is also interesting to see how the shareholders view this. For example, do they honor the additional 20% or do they punish the 90%?

Furthermore, we cannot always achieve all goals at once or in one step: If at first the restoration of the unity of the Union was the primary goal of his first presidency of Abraham Lincoln, towards the end of the Civil War Lincoln was able to push through the Emancipation Proclamation to free all American slaves (a goal that in 1861 was also not yet communicable to all his North American supporters, see Nagler 2015). In this context, entrepreneurs can sometimes plan better for the long term and have more room to maneuver than CEOs of stock corporations, as CEOs have to pay more attention to the quarterly figures (e.g., the share price).

Finally, we would like to venture an outlook: The **ability to learn**, to **innovate** and to be **capable of change** in general should always be **combined with** a certain **serenity**: we now call this **business**

serenity management (we liked the series "Firefly" with the spaceship "Serenity"):

- Learn the serenity of a Buddhist monk, a doctor in a life-changing surgery (many thanks to my surgeons), a good captain in a storm (we're thinking of our father-in-law/grandpa Daniel, who survived a terrible typhoon in the South China Sea as a young first officer), or a manager in a complicated negotiation.
- Take the world as it really is (see Stockdale paradox); change it (within the limits where that is even possible).

And one last point: let's bring trust and fun back into the game! And one thing is certain: the story is not over yet.

"Success is never final and failure never fatal. It's courage that counts" (allegedly Winston Churchill, presumably the quote comes from other sources such as a Budweiser beer advertisement from the 1930s, see https://quoteinvestigator. com/2013/09/03/success-final/ Status: August 2024).

Comments and Conclusions

"What would you do if you had a million dollars?" (Dialogue between Ron Livingston aka Peter and Diedrich Bader aka Lawrence in "Office Space"; 1999 film by Mike Judge): Peter: "Nothing." Laurence: "Nothing, huh?" Peter: "I would relax. I would sit on my ass all day. I would do nothing." Laurence: "You don't need a million dollars to do nothing. Take a look at my cousin. He's broke, don't do shit."

Our personal and organization's vision and mission and our self-set goals are crucial for a successful future. The question of how we measure success and which criteria we use must be answered individually by each person (or organization). A salesman will most certainly understand this to mean profit (e.g., through the sale of the Eiffel Tower), a developer the number of patents granted (e.g., for a perpetual motion machine) and a treasure hunter being the first to find El Dorado or Cibola. Furthermore, our motives and our goals including our vision do not have to appear at all insightful or even reasonable to others. It is and remains our life, our organization and our decision; but also, our responsibility!

"When I go home and people ask me: 'Hey, Hoot, why do you do it, man? Why? You some kind of war junkie?' I won't say a goddamn word. Why? They won't understand. They won't understand why we do it. They won't understand it's about the men next to you. And that's it. That's all it is" (Eric Bana alias Sergeant First Class Norm "Hoot" Gibson in "Black Hawk Down").

Being successful is absolutely important for an organization, but it's also not everything in life. Above all, success also depends on one's perspective. Certain people and organizations may well be considered successful by us, but they themselves would possibly evaluate this completely differently. And vice versa. We should also remember that at the very least, our priorities can change (e.g., being a good company, intending now to become a top company). Furthermore, certain successes that seemed important to us when we were young may seem secondary when we get older. The overarching question then becomes: **What is really important?** It is therefore not surprising that Schur and Weick also pose the question of meaning at the end of their book about career. Of course, they are not the first to ask this question or to have dealt with the question of meaning. We have already quoted or mentioned philosophers and writers such as Emperor Marcus Aurelius, Niccolò Machiavelli and Viktor Frankl several times. At this point, of course, we do not want to and cannot answer the question of meaning in life, but at least we can refer to their works.

"... That those were still most capable of surviving even such borderline situations – those, I say, who were oriented toward the future, toward a task that awaited them, toward a meaning that they wanted to fulfill" in "Der Mensch vor der Frage nach dem Sinn" (Frankl 2019, freely translated).

"Meaning cannot be given, but must be found. And indeed, this process of this finding of sense amounts to a Gestalt perception ... Sense must be found, but cannot be generated. What can be generated is either subjective sense, a mere sense feeling, or – nonsense ... But sense must not only be found, but can be found, and in the search for it man is guided by conscience. In a word, the conscience is a sense organ" in "Der Mensch vor der Frage nach dem Sinn" (Frankl 2019, freely translated).

"So, every day, every hour waits with a new meaning, and another meaning waits for every man" ... "In the fulfillment of meaning man realizes himself. If we fulfill only the sense of suffering, we realize the most human thing in man, we mature, we grow beyond ourselves. Just there, where we are helpless and hopeless insofar as we cannot change a situation – just there we are called upon and are demanded to change ourselves" in "Der Mensch vor der Frage nach dem Sinn" (Frankl 2019, freely translated).

"... For it is the duty of a righteous man to teach others the good which he has not been able to perform because of the adversity of times and fate, so that among many capable ones, one whom Heaven loves more may carry it out" (Machiavelli in the Discorsi, Book 2, Preface, freely translated).

If we have put the **question of meaning** on hold for a while, or even if we have answered it satisfactorily for ourselves, one question remains: What is the secret of success? In a nutshell, it is the identified individual and general success factors (see pages 120-123, see also the previous chapters), but above all the proper management of the remaining TO DOs (i.e., implementation), see previous two chapters and next table.

1	Ask yourself: **What am I passionate about?** See also Papa-Rolf-Benno principle or the Hedgehog concept (see Collins)
2	**Focus on Business Concept Innovation** (see Hamel and Prahalad), do not focus exclusively on technology alone (see Collins)
3	**Help Clients Succeed** (see Khalsa)
4	**Develop a sense of opportunity** (see Khalsa and Senger: kairos, serendipity); **focus on / put the best people on opportunities, not on problems** (see Collins, Drucker, see also Moltke and Sunzi)
5	**Furthermore, never leave anything to chance if one could influence it oneself** (see Lincoln, Schur and Weick)
6	**Apply risk management correctly** (see Drucker, Sunzi or Moltke)
7	**Develop list sensitivity** (in the sense of the 36 stratagems)
8	**Pay attention to effectiveness** (which is more important than efficiency). **Do the right things right: at the right time in the right order** (see Collins, Covey, Drucker and Grant; see also Clausewitz, Moltke and Sunzi)
9	**Focus on feasibility** (see Drucker, Musashi, Moltke and Sunzi)
10	**Think holistically** (see Pink – right & left brainer; DevOps, Design and Process School, BANWAD and TUDAPOL); "No Tyranny of the OR / Genius of the AND"
11	**Remain adaptable and transformable** (see Darwin, Machiavelli and Westkämper)
12	**Master your Upper Limit Problem** (see Hendricks); don't settle for average
13	**Develop Level 5 leadership and a Culture of discipline** (see Collins)
14	**First WHO, then WHAT** (see Collins) → Get the right people on board
15	**"Be in the center of power"** (see Schur and Weick)
16	**It's a people business: Be good TO and WITH people**

Table: Our guidelines for success (Remaining TO Dos). Note: This is not a complete "checklist". There will "never" be such a list!

Not every idea presented here is recommended specifically for us or is even (sensibly and profitably) implementable or desirable for us and for our organization. However, we should know the different options, concepts and ideas leading to success. In this regard, we should especially remember Musashi, who not only expects success just by the surprising change of methods and tools, but furthermore gives the following to consider: "In the fight for life and death one should use every weapon, because to die with an unused weapon in the belt would be senseless".

***

We would like to comment briefly on our point of view. When we think of Collins' assessment regarding the importance of technology, we are still debating to what extent it is accurate. Technology alone is of course not enough to be successful or to become a top (i.e., a good-to-great) company. Nevertheless, certain companies in the high-tech or pharmaceutical industries would undoubtedly not be where they are now without R&D and technology. Likewise, think of the R&D organizations, IT giants, the aerospace or automotive industries, and all the hidden champions in machinery and equipment manufacturing.

Moreover, we are still convinced that clear, committed goals (and the strategies derived from them) are absolutely crucial for success and that at least company founders and entrepreneurs must have a (crystal-clear) vision right from the start. The Wright Brothers, for example, were driven by their vision of flying, without which they would not likely have been able to realize their dream against all odds and build an aerospace company. We should therefore not forget that the advice (First WHO, then WHAT) is addressed mainly to existing companies that want to become a top company. A last word on First WHO, then WHAT: The rule here is that the common sharing of goals and values is more important than the technical training of employees. Knowledge gaps can be closed with a little effort. Fundamental "cultural" differences (in discipline, work ethic, etc.) tend not to be eliminated or they need a lot of time and effort which we maybe do not have (note: it took several decades to develop and implement lean thinking in the automotive industry). Hence, why we must not make false compromises in our choice of employees. As Collins said, "Don't hire ... keep looking" (Collins 2020). We should really take the issue of probation seriously.

And much is relative: There is often no either-or, as Mintzberg already recognized in relation to organizations. We therefore believe that a holistic approach, i.e., a compromise between Process School and Design School, is helpful and even imperative (Ritter 2013).

We should also pay more attention to the factors of chance and luck. At least these factors should not be completely ignored in our calculations (see "Fog of War", Clausewitz 2003 and Sunzi 2001): We are often forced to take decisions based on incomplete information. Thus, we need to cope with the related risks, e.g., by thinking in scenarios (e.g., worst-case-scenario, best-case-scenario, see also Ritter 2013). Freelancers, start-up founders and small business owners should definitely keep this in mind.

With regard to personal success, we must not neglect one factor either: Of course, we can't control our individual starting conditions (e.g., our genes, place of birth, social circumstances and IQ factor). Let us therefore focus on the things that we can influence. In this respect, we find the Hedgehog concept (Collins) or the Papa-Rolf-Benno principle to be quite fundamental; above all the question: What am I passionate about?

Even though we are not all the same (many companies are also unique in their own way) – there is still one approach that each of us can take to become even more successful (see also strategic stretch and resource leverage): mastering our individual "Upper Limit Problem". It is comparable to a journey in a hot-air balloon. And "there are driving forces that cannot be influenced by us, such as storms, but also coincidences or the physical world. Even our lives are more like a balloon than an airship" (Ritter 2021).

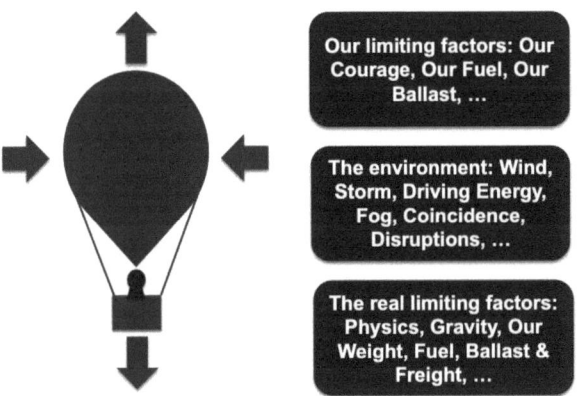

Figure: The Balloonist Model for success (Ritter 2021)

We are firmly convinced that each of us can individually push our personal limits. This does not mean striving for perfection. The desire for perfection can even become rather hindering or not worth the effort. Reducing complexity (e.g., through simplification, see also page 40 and Ritter 2020) and the Pareto principle (80/20 rule) are a promising approach. In addition, effectiveness is much more important to us than efficiency.

If we were to provide a **minimal model for success**, we would draw the final conclusion:

1) **think strategic,**
2) **develop a sense of serendipity and**
3) **serenity**.

These are the **three virtues of success** for us.

	Virtue		Scope
1	Strategic thinking	Focus on	... the individual and strategic success factors, value creation (e.g., Arnold's Value-Action Pentagon Model) and feasibility (see Musashi and Moltke)
		Develop	... a clear vision, agree on clear goals and develop a sense for entrepreneurship / intrapreneurship (including Business Concept Innovation)
		Understand	... the difference of Design and Process School. The development of strategies is a holistic, integrative, never-ending approach. Therefore, think like a Strategic Control Loop and consider control theory (i.e., stability, damping, quick response, state stationary control precision and robustness)
		Consider	... powerful concepts like the Basic Strategy Concept (see pages 14 and 73) or the TUDAPOL principle (Think Unlimited, Develop Agile, Produce and Operate Lean)
2	Sense of Serendipity	Focus on	... the success factors and start to think beyond (see BANWAD way: Beyond Agile, New Work and Digitalization)
		Develop	... a sense for opportunities and chances (kairos, pain & gain). Furthermore, one should never leave anything to chance if one could influence it oneself
		Understand	... the business context and the difference between pain & gain and opportunities & problems we should not solve: Look for opportunities rather than problems (focus on strengths rather than weaknesses, see Drucker)
		Consider	... powerful concepts like the ORDER principle, the Hedgehog concept and the Papa-Rolf-Benno principle
3	Sense of Serenity	Focus on	... the individual and strategic success factors. Don't forget Stonewall Jackson: "Never take counsel of your fears". Focus on your Zone of Excellence and Zone of Genius. Forget any type of dogmatism!
		Develop	... a sense for balancing (e.g., activity versus passivity, effectiveness versus efficiency, ...): "No Tyranny of the OR / Genius of the AND". Develop your leadership skills
		Understand	... stratagems and your Upper Limit Problem and challenge it
		Consider	... powerful concepts like the Change Kaleidoscope and the Papa Daniel Rule

Table: Triple-S-Virtues for Success Approach

Last Words

> "(1) If you find something better in human life than justice, truth, self-control, courage, and, in a word, satisfaction of your mind with itself, as far as it lets you act according to right reason, and satisfaction with destiny in everything; if, therefore, I say, you see something better, turn to it with all your soul and enjoy what you have found to be the best" (Marcus Aurelius in his Self-Reflections – Third Book, 6 (1), freely translated).

The list of success factors will probably never be complete. The concepts and ideas discussed in this book serve as a stimulus. Their application does not necessarily guarantee success, their incorrect application does not necessarily guarantee failure. Our lives, our markets and our world are far too complex and turbulent for that. As Udo Lindenberg sings in his film "Lindenberg! Do your thing": "... There are no street signs in the jungle. You have to find your own way". In addition, and this can be observed again and again in successful people such as Abraham Lincoln as one of the most important U.S. presidents, Arnold Schwarzenegger as a professional bodybuilder, businessman, filmmaker and governor of California or Udo Lindenberg as a German singer, composer and painter, a steadfast will to win and confidence in the sense of Musashi, Sunzi, Moltke or the Stockdale paradox are essential:

> "... I never doubted that I would get through this. I never doubted I could do it. I've always known that I could do the top things. Never doubted it, I can do it. It's clear, I can manage it" (Udo Lindenberg in his song sung in the film "Lindenberg! Mach dein Ding" song "Niemals dran gezweifelt", freely translated).

Being successful is all well and good. However, we should not forget other important aspects, as Arnold Schwarzenegger critically summarizes when looking back on his successful career and business life:

> "There's a mission. Now some people take seminars about this stuff, how to feel better about all this stuff, but I always tell people: **Stay busy. Be useful!**" (Arnold Schwarzenegger in the documentary miniseries "Arnold", part 3, see Chilcott 2023).

If we are aware of the appropriate, fundamental success factors, this can help us to think the right things and do the right things right for us and our organizations. To put it in a nutshell, we need to acquire the following virtues:

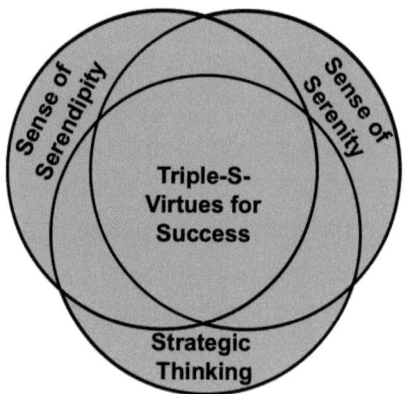

Figure: Triple-S-Virtues for Success

There remains the often too seldom followed advice:

"Tun!" (i.e., "Do!"); see "Klaus Killmann Rule", page 116

In this spirit, we wish you a good portion of serenity and a lot of fun in the sense of the Papa-Rolf-Benno principle. We wish you and your organizations all the best in becoming successful successfully.

Arno Ritter
Hamburg, Germany, Summer 2024

Roderick Ritter
Taipei, Taiwan, Summer 2024

Glossary

Agile Management: management style based on the agile values (i.e., courage, commitment, focus, openness, and respect) and on strong customer focus, iterative approach and empowered teams; see also Agile Manifesto (preference of individuals and interaction over processes and tools, functional products over documentation, collaboration with the customer over contracts, and changeability over just following plans).

Agile Manifesto:

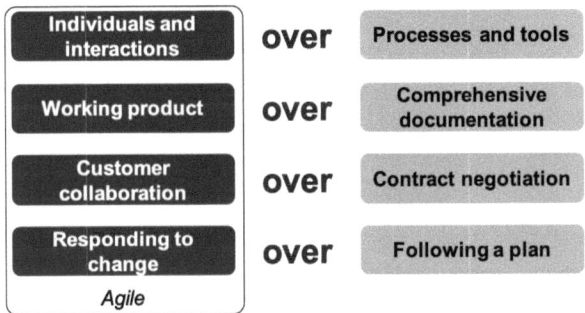

Figure: The Agile Manifesto = A philosophy with a set of values

Agile Principles:

Iterations	The products are developed in a step-by-step approach. At the end of each step, feedback is given by the customer.
Increments	At the end of each iteration, a working product is presented to the customer.
Simplicity	Only activities that are really needed are performed.
Readiness for change	The request for changes is seen as something normal and is seen as an opportunity.
Reviews	The customer is regularly involved. Interim results are regularly presented. The progress is transparent. He is able to give feedback.
Retrospectives	Apart from the progress review, the development process and the collaboration are regularly reviewed. The result is the continuous improvement of the way of working and collaboration.
Self-organizing teams	Teams are autonomous and self-organizing. They take responsibility for their work and their results and increase the efficiency of their way of working.
Cooperation (experts & developers)	Misunderstandings and inefficiency within the collaboration are minimized by close cooperation and clear and transparent communication.

Figure: Important agile principles according to Preußig (2015), see Ritter (2020)

Arnold's Value-Action Pentagon Model: model according to Arnold, focusing on the areas where "Value" can be generated: 1) Projects with positive and high Net Profit Value; 2) Our Investment Portfolio; 3) Divestment; 4) Life Cycle Extension; 5) Retain Profit.

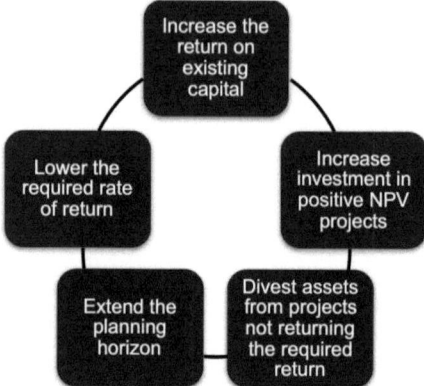

Figure: Value-Action Pentagon Model according to Arnold (Neale and McElroy 2004)

Auftragstaktik (mission command): a concept introduced by Helmuth von Moltke (in continuity with the work of Scharnhorst, Clausewitz and Müffling); i.e., emphasizing the outcome of a mission rather than the specific means to achieve it. The concept is more accurately described by its contemporary definition as "Führen durch Auftrag" (i.e., leading by mission). This approach has been a central component of the military tactics (and successes) of the German armed forces since the 19th century and was later successfully adopted and applied by the Israel Defense Forces. The military leader specifies the objective, usually the time frame and the required forces. On the basis of these framework conditions, the leader tasked with the mission pursues and achieves the objective independently and flexibly. "Management by Objectives" (Peter Drucker) or "Planned Opportunism" (Jack Welch) could be seen as its counterpart in business.

A Whole New Mind – Why Right-Brainers Will Rule the Future: book by Daniel Pink about success by focusing on the so-called "Six Senses": design, story, symphony, empathy, play, and meaning.

BANWAD (Beyond Agile, New Work and Digitalization): (our) concept to meet the challenges of the future (New Work, Digitalization and Agility/Agile Management).

B	Beyond	• MANAGING AND MASTERING … ○ THE STABILITY AND TRANSFORMABILTY CHALLENGE ○ THE INNOVATION CHALLENGE ○ THE COMPLEXITY CHALLENGE ○ THE BALANCE CHALLENGE ○ THE IMPLEMENTATION CHALLENGE

A	Agile	<ul><li>Agile Values like commitment</li><li>Minimum Viable Product</li><li>Fast decision-making</li><li>The "D-A" in the TUDAPOL principle</li></ul>
N	New	<ul><li>New mindset (think of Design, Story, Symphony, Empathy, Play, Meaning), see "Six Senses"</li><li>No straitjacket in thinking (The "T-U" in the TUDAPOL principle)</li><li>Respect for the individuum and conscious and real leadership: courage, trust, respect, openness, focus, commitment, learning, innovation, creating space</li></ul>
W	Work	<ul><li>Flexibility & New Work concepts</li><li>The "T-U", "D-A" and "P-O-L" in the TUDAPOL principle. It is a people business!</li></ul>
A	And	<ul><li>Success factors (& Leadership)</li><li>(Strategy) Framework and Strategic Control Loop</li><li>The TUDAPOL principle</li></ul>
D	Digitalization	<ul><li>Enabler & opportunity</li></ul>

Table: The B-A-N-W-A-D-WAY (a brief summary), see Ritter 2021

Bryson, William "Bill": American-British travel writer and author of popular science books such as "A Short History of Nearly Everything" (2003).

Built to Last: the book based on a six-year research project (1994) by Jim Collins and Jerry I. Porras on the underlying success principles for lasting business success.

Burry, Michael James: an American investor, hedge fund manager (founder of Scion Capital), and physician who predicted and profited from the mortgage crisis that occurred between 2007 and 2010 (see also the biographical comedy-drama "The Big Short").

Business Concept Innovation (according to Hamel and Prahalad): in contrast to innovative products, services and processes, the innovative design of a business model.

Business Model: in general, the description of the way an organization functions and the underlying concept of generating profits. Examples: Free(mium), multi-sided platforms, or digital business models.

Business Model Canvas (according to Osterwalder and Pigneur): simple concept and method for analyzing and defining business models. The model can be sketched on a "canvas", focusing on our "value proposition" (our value proposition to our customers) and contrasting the "cost structure" (with the "key resources", "key activities" and "key partners" required for our value proposition), with the "revenue streams" (with the "channels", "customer relationships" and the "customer segments" defined for this purpose).

Business Serenity Management: (our) vision of a future, "more relaxed" management style with a focus on people without misguided dogmatism, see also Ritter (2021) and "Triple-S-Virtues for Success".

Change Kaleidoscope (according to Balogun and Hope Hailey): process model and framework for analyzing and designing change.

Clausewitz, Carl von (* July 1, 1780; † November 16, 1831): Prussian major general and army reformer; one of the most important military scientists, philosophers and ethicists; main work: "Vom Kriege" ("On War").

Collins, Jim: internationally known management expert and author of "Good to Great" and "Built to Last".

Conscious leadership: a concept developed by Jim Dethmer, Diana Chapman and Kaley Warner Klemp in their book "The 15 Commitments of Conscious Leadership: A New Paradigm for Sustainable Success".

Control loop: a control loop is a dynamic system or the dynamic process of action between controller and controlled system for influencing the controlled variable in a closed system, in which this variable is continuously measured and continuously compared with the reference variable. An important factor here is the negative feedback of the current value of the controlled variable. The deviation of the actual value from the reference variable is continuously (counter)acted upon by the controller on the controlled system in the sense of an adjustment. Examples: air conditioning and cruise control.

Covey, Stephen R. (* October 24, 1932; † July 16, 2012): U.S. best-selling author of self-help books and university lecturer; author of "The Seven Habits of Highly Effective People" – one of the most influential management books of modern times.

Criteria for successful strategies: (our) basic success factors for strategies, such as can be derived from our experience and the works of Clausewitz, Grant and Sunzi, see Ritter (2013, 2020 and 2021).

Cultural Web: this framework, which goes back to Johnson and Scholes, enables the analysis and design of organizations in the context of "change" according to the (technical) dimension (organizational structures, control system), its political dimension (formal and informal power structures) and its cultural manifestation (routines, rituals, "stories" and symbols).

Darwin, Robert Charles (* February 12, 1809; † April 19, 1882): British natural scientist who is considered one of the most important natural scientists of the modern era due to his contribution to the theory of evolution (e.g., gradualism, origin of species). Famous is his participation in the expedition of the HMS Beagle to the Galapagos Islands.

De Geus, Arie: Dutch manager, speaker and economic theorist; former head of Royal Dutch Shell's Strategic Planning Group.

Denominator management (according to Hamel): the reduction of costs (denominator) as opposed to the increase of value or growth (numerator). Denominator management is a common, but not really sustainable strategic measure. For a short moment, the balance sheet looks good, but it does not create new products, new services, new markets, or new value. Hamel warns against this! Downsizing is the opposite of growth.

Der abenteuerliche Simplicissimus Teutsch: the first German adventure novel (in the sense of the "low" genre of the picaresque novel). The "Simplicissimus", published in 1668 by Hans Jakob Christoph von Grimmelshausen, is one of the most significant works of the Baroque in the German language and describes quite drastically the age of the Thirty Years' War (1618–48) and contains one of the first Robinsonades in world literature (50 years before the appearance of Robinson Crusoe). As Volker Meid writes, "This great picaresque novel of the Baroque combines popular and scholarly traditions in a unique way, and thanks to its realistic language and astonishing fullness of life, it is still today – as the Baroque title page already promised – 'exceedingly funny and manly to read'."

Design School (also Rational School or Planning School): theory according to which strategy development primarily has a planning character. For the Design School, the focus of strategy development is on a structured, analytical approach.

Design Thinking: holistic, interdisciplinary approach based on a set of cognitive, strategic and practical procedures used by designers in the process of designing; transferred to innovation management; including creative thinking, solution-focused thinking, prototyping, end-user testing, etc.

DevOps: a holistic, integrative concept for (software) development, which encompasses development and operation.

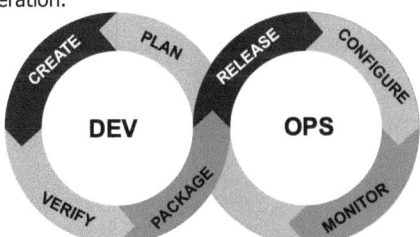

Figure: The Software Development Life Cycle "Changing Processes: From a Line to a Circuit" (Freeman 2019)

Discorsi (Conversations): Machiavelli's fundamental work on politics and the state. Machiavelli deals with the only partially surviving works of Titus Livius on the history of early Roman history and transfers his insights to modern times. According to Horst Günther: "It is a wonderful book of trust in reason".

Drucker, Peter Ferdinand (* November 19, 1909; † November 11, 2005): Austrian-U.S. economist and pioneer of modern management theory; often called the "father of modern management". Author of "The Effective Executive"; introduced, among other things, the concept of "management by objectives", the "concept of core competence", and the "knowledge worker".

Efficient-Market Hypothesis: economic hypothesis which states that share prices reflect all available (market) information. It would therefore be impossible to "beat the market" in the long term. Remark: Warren Buffett is critical of this theory.

Eisenhower, Dwight David "Ike" (* October 14, 1890; † March 28, 1969): U.S. general and, during World War II, Supreme Commander of the Supreme Headquarters, Allied Expeditionary Force in Europe; from 1953 to 1961, the thirty-fourth U.S. president.

Eisenhower Matrix (method or principle): method attributed to General Eisenhower of categorizing tasks by urgency (urgent/not urgent) and importance (important/not important): 1) Important/urgent: do yourself immediately. 2) Important/not urgent: schedule and complete yourself. 3) Not important/urgent: delegate to competent employees. 4) Not important/not urgent: do not process (wastebasket). Criticism (see also Covey): recognition that important tasks are rarely urgent and urgent tasks are rarely important.

Emergent Strategy: according to Henry Mintzberg, the strategy later realized in an organization is not only the result of rational planning of strategies, but emergent strategies that were not written down anywhere, but have evolved out of the enterprise. Comment: serendipity can be a major driver in this process.

Empowerment: achieved state of self-determination and self-responsibility, or strategies and actions designed to increase the degree of autonomy and self-determination in the lives of people or communities.

Frankl, Viktor Emil (* March 26, 1905; † September 2, 1997): one of the most important neurologists and psychiatrists after Sigmund Freud and a survivor of the Holocaust. Frankl founded the so-called logotherapy and existential analysis, often referred to as the "Third Viennese School of Psychotherapy". One of his best-known works is "... trotzdem Ja zum Leben sagen: Ein Psychologe erlebt das Konzentrationslager / Man's Search for Meaning" (1946).

Fraunhofer-Gesellschaft: named after Joseph von Fraunhofer (a Bavarian scientist, engineer and entrepreneur); it is the largest organization for applied research and development services in Europe. The so-called "Fraunhofer model" is based on 30% funding from the German federal and state governments and 70% of income from industrial and public projects.

Genghis Khan date test: "Ask a group to write down the last 3 digits of their phone numbers, and then ask them to estimate the date of Genghis Khan's death. Time and again, the results show a correlation between the two numbers; people assume that he lived in the first millennium, when in fact he lived from 1162 to 1227" (Roxburgh 2003).

Good to Great: the book based on the study of 1500 Fortune 500 companies published in 2001, in which Jim Collins and his team investigated the question of how a company could become a top company.

Gneisenau, August Wilhelm Anton Neidhardt von (* October 27, 1760; † August 23, 1831): Field Marshal and reformer of the Prussian army; one of the main German protagonists in the victory over Napoleon (e.g., battle of Waterloo).

Grant, Robert: management professor and author of "Contemporary strategy analysis – concepts, techniques, applications"; typical representative of the Design School.

Guderian, Heinz Wilhelm (* June 17, 1888; † May 14, 1954): colonel general and "inventor" of the German tank force as an independent troop type; proponent of the tactical concept "battle of combined arms" and "command from the front"; author of the non-fiction book "Achtung – Panzer!" (1937).

Günther, Horst: German philosopher, translator, editor and author specializing in the philosophy of history and political theory.

Hamel, Gary: management professor and author of "Leading the Revolution – How to Thrive in Turbulent Times by Making Innovation a Way of Life" and "Competing for the future". Hamel introduced the term "Business Concept Innovation", "Resource leverage" and "Strategic stretch".

Harari, Yuval Noah: internationally known historian and author of popular science works such as "A Brief History of Mankind" and "Homo Deus. A History of Tomorrow".

Hendricks, Gay: psychologist, professor and author of "THE BIG LEAP: Conquer Your Hidden Fear and Take Life to the Next Level".

Heraclitus of Ephesus (circa * 535 B.C., circa † 475 B.C.): native of the city of Ephesus; an ancient Greek, pre-Socratic philosopher; called the "the obscure".

Il Principe ("The Prince"): the best-known work of Machiavelli, written around 1513 and dedicated to Lorenzo di Piero de' Medici, which is considered one of the first and most important works of modern state philosophy.

Implementation: implementation here (in this book) usually means the implementation (i.e., definition, development and realization) of (successful) strategies.

Innovation: in the economic sense, one can only speak of an innovation – in contrast to a pure invention – when its usefulness is recognized and a product/service, business process or business model is introduced or changed accordingly. Robert Grant basically distinguishes between product innovation, process innovation and strategic innovation. Furthermore, Peter Drucker distinguishes between product, social and management innovation (i.e., innovation of products and services, customer behavior and values, innovation of capabilities and activities to produce and market products and services).

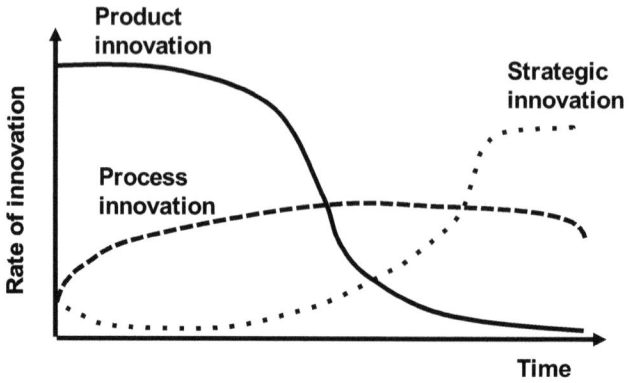

Figure: The three types of innovations (Grant 2002)

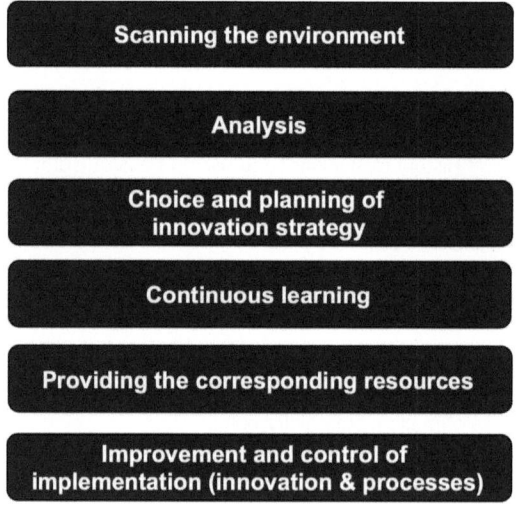

Table: The innovation process according to Brown et al. (2002)

Ishikawa diagrams (according to Kaoru Ishikawa; also called fishbone diagrams, cause-and-effect diagrams): causal diagrams that show the potential causes (environment, machines, materials, measurements, methods, personnel) of a specific event (i.e., problem/issue).

Jackson, Thomas Jonathan (* January 21, 1824; † May 10, 1863): American Civil War general in the Confederate States Army; called "Stonewall" because of his steadfastness at the First Battle of Bull Run (also Battle of Manassas); considered "General Robert E. Lee's most able subordinate".

Kaizen: continuous improvement; key element of lean management, see also Lean Lexicon.

Kroc, Raymond Albert (* October 5, 1902; † January 14, 1984): the so-called "Hamburger King" was founder and CEO of McDonald's Corporation. Representing kitchen equipment (such as a multi-mixer), he visited brothers Richard "Dick" and Maurice "Mac" McDonald at their burger restaurant in San Bernardino, California, after receiving a major order (six milkshake mixers) and immediately recognized the potential of their restaurant concept with its perfected, standardized workflows, "site" design, reduced lead times, standardized products, consistent quality, reduced costs (e.g., by using disposable packaging materials) etc. (see Lean Management and Lean Thinking). He acquired the franchise rights, opened his first McDonald's restaurant in Des Plaines, Illinois, and later expanded around the world on the basis of the successful concept.

Lateral Thinking (according to Edward de Bono): problem solving using an indirect and creative approach via reasoning that is not immediately obvious (e.g., by provocation).

Lean Lexicon: important definitions for **Lean Manufacturing** and **Lean Management**.

Continuous Flow	Producing and moving one item at a time (or a small and consistent batch of items) through a series of processing steps as continuously as possible, with each step making just what is requested by the next step. Continuous flow can be achieved in a number of ways, ranging from moving assembly lines to manual cells. It is also called **one-piece flow, single-piece flow**, and **make one, move one**.
Cycle Time	How often a part or product is actually completed by a process, as timed by observation. Also, the time it takes an operator to go through all work elements before repeating them.
Error-Proofing	Methods that help operators avoid mistakes in their work caused by choosing the wrong part, leaving out a part, installing a part backwards, etc. Also, called **mistake-proofing, poka-yoke (error-proofing)** and **baka-yoke (fool-proofing)**.
First In, First Out (FIFO)	The principle and practice of maintaining precise production and conveyance sequence by ensuring that the first part to enter a process or storage location is also the first part to exit. FIFO is a necessary condition for pull system implementation.
Five Ss (Japanese)	**Seiri:** Separate needed from unneeded items – tools, parts, materials, paperwork – and discard the unneeded. **Seiton:** Neatly arrange what is left – a place for everything and everything in its place.

	Seiso: Clean and wash. **Seiketsu:** Cleanliness resulting from regular performance of the first three Ss. **Shitsuke:** Discipline to perform the first four Ss.
Five Ss (English)	**Sifting (Seiri):** Go through everything in the work area, separating and eliminating what isn't needed. **Sorting (Seiton):** Arrange items that are needed in a neat and easy-to-use manner. **Sweeping clean (Seiso):** Clean up the work area, equipment and tools. **Spic and Span (Seiketsu):** The overall cleanliness and order that result from disciplined practice of the first three Ss. **Sustain (Shitsuke):** Mostly dropped because it becomes redundant under Toyota's system of daily, weekly, and monthly audits to check standardized work.
Heijunka	**Leveling the type and quantity** of production over a fixed period of time. This enables production of efficiently meet customer demands while avoiding batching and results in minimum inventories, capital costs, manpower, and production lead time through the whole value stream.
Jidoka	Providing machines and operators the ability to detect when an abnormal condition has occurred and immediately stop work.
Just-in-Time (JIT) Production	A system of production that makes and delivers just what is needed, just when it is needed, and just in the amount needed. JIT and Jidoka are two pillars of the Toyota Production System. **JIT relies on Heijunka** as foundation and is comprised of three operating elements: the pull system, takt time, and continuous flow.
Kaizen	**Continuous improvement** of an entire value stream or an individual process to create more value with less waste.
Kanban	A kanban is a signaling device that gives authorization and instructions for the production or withdrawal (conveyance) of items in a pull system. The term is Japanese for "sign" or "signboard".
Lean Production	A business system for organizing and managing product development, operations, suppliers, and customer relations that requires less human effort, less space, less capital, and less time to make products with fewer defects to precise customer desires, compared with the previous system of mass production. Lean production was pioneered by Toyota after World War II.
Lean Thinking	A **five-step thought process** proposed by Womack and Jones: 1.) Specify value from the standpoint of the end customer by product family. 2.) Identify all the steps in the value stream for each product family, eliminating whenever possible those steps that do not create value. 3.) Make the value creating steps occur in tight sequence so the product will flow smoothly toward the customer.

	4.) As flow is introduced, let customers pull value from the next upstream activity. 5.) As value is specified, value streams are identified, wasted steps are removed, and flow and pull are introduced, begin the process again and continue it until a state of perfection is reached in which perfect value is created with no waste.
Muda, Mura, Muri	Three terms often used together in the Toyota Production System (and called **Three Ms**) that collectively describe wasteful practices to be eliminated. • **Muda:** any activity that consumes resources without creating value for the customer. • **Mura:** unevenness in operation • **Muri:** overburdening equipment or operators by requiring them to run at a higher or harder pace with more force and effort for longer period of time than equipment designs and appropriate workforce management allow.
Production Lead Time	The time it takes one piece to move all the way through a process or a value stream, from start to finish. Envision timing a market part as it moves from beginning to end.
Production Kanban	Tell an upstream process the type and quantity of products to make for the downstream process. In the simplest situation, a card corresponds to one container of parts, which the upstream process will make for the supermarket ahead of the next downstream process.
Pull system	A method of production control in which downstream activities signal their needs to upstream activities. Pull production strives to eliminate overproduction and is one of the three major components of a complete JIT production system.
Seven Wastes	Taichi Ohno's categorization of the seven major wastes typically found in mass production: 1.) **Overproduction:** Production ahead of what's actually needed by the next process or customer. The worst form of waste because it contributes to the other six. 2.) **Waiting:** Operators standing idle as machine cycle, equipment fails, needed parts fail to arrive, etc. 3.) **Conveyance:** Moving parts and products unnecessarily, such as from a processing step to a warehouse to a subsequent processing step when the second step could be located instead immediately adjacent to the first step. 4.) **Processing:** Performing unnecessary or incorrect processing, typically from poor tool or product design. 5.) **Inventory:** Having more than the minimum stocks necessary for a precisely controlled pull system. 6.) **Motion:** Operators making movements that are straining or unnecessary, such as looking for parts, tools, documents, etc. 7.) **Correction:** Inspection, rework, and scrap.
Takt time	The available production time divided by customer demand.

Value	The inherent worth of a product as judgement by the customer and reflected in its selling price and market demand.
Value Creating Time	Time of those work elements that actually transform the product in a way that the customer is willing to pay for.
Value stream	All of the actions, both value-creating and non-value-creating, required to bring a product from concept to launch and from order to delivery. These include actions to process information from the customer and actions to transform the product on its way to the customer.

Table: Lean Lexicon - The Lean Enterprise Institute (2003)

Lean Management: totality of principles, methods and procedures for the efficient design of the entire value chain, see also Toyota Production System, based on concepts such as standardization, elimination of waste, continuous improvement or continuous flow.

Lincoln, Abraham (* February 12, 1809; † April 15, 1865): as the sixteenth U.S. president, steered the Union through the American Civil War (1861–1865) and restored the unity of the United States lost by the secession of the Confederate States. The Emancipation Proclamation (and the Thirteenth Amendment to the Constitution) freed over four million slaves. Lincoln became the first U.S. president to fall victim to an assassination attempt by a fanatical Southerner only a short time after the victorious end of the Civil War. Lincoln was regarded as a self-taught, self-made man, meticulous worker and good networker who, through his human nature and great sense of humor, was able to win over a large number of people to himself and his vision of a united, free and modern America.

Lindenberg, Udo (* May 17, 1946): German singer, drummer, and composer. Lindenberg created a new style of new German-language music, finding a niche between internationally oriented Krautrock and mainstream pop music.

Machiavelli, Niccolò (* May 3, 1469; † June 21, 1527): Italian poet, philosopher, chronicler and diplomat of his home town Florence; one of the most important state philosophers of modern times; author of the "Principe" ("The Prince") and the "Discorsi" ("Conversations").

Mackenzie, Alec: internationally known speaker, consultant and expert on time management; author of "The Time Trap: The Classic Book on Time Management".

Manstein, Fritz Erich von (* November 24, 1887; † June 10, 1973): German field marshal; convicted as a war criminal in 1949 and the only former field marshal to serve until 1960 as an unofficial advisor to the German government on the reestablishment of a new army; devised the plan, reminiscent of the Schlieffen Plan, to conquer France (later called the "sickle cut" by Winston Churchill) in violation of international law and the neutrality of the Benelux countries.

Manufacturing execution system (MES): computer-based systems (partially in real-time) for the management and control of resources (e.g., personnel, machinery, inputs) in manufacturing, e.g., for resource scheduling, order execution and dispatch, production analysis, etc. (i.e., track and document the transformation of raw materials to finished goods).

Marcus Aurelius (* April 26, 121; † March 17, 180): from March 7, 161 until his death, the last of the so-called "adopted emperors" (succeeding Emperor Hadrian and Antoninus Pius); the "philosopher on the imperial throne" is considered one of the most important and respected Roman emperors. Prussian king Frederick the Great and statesmen such as Bill Clinton and Helmut Schmidt counted him among their role models.

Mell, Heiko: German personnel consultant, book author and freelancer for VDI nachrichten; since 1984, he has been responsible for the "Career Advice" series for decades.

Minimum Viable Product: a configuration of a saleable and usable product/service that can be further expanded in the sense of the lean start-up concept. A Minimum Viable Product should enable the fastest possible customer and user feedback in order to prevent undesirable developments (and minimize risks) and to enable new requirements to be met more quickly. A Minimum Viable Product requires a "generic architecture".

Mintzberg, Henry: internationally known management professor and author of "The Strategy Process"; typical representative of the Process School.

Moltke, Helmuth Karl Bernhard von (* October 26, 1800; † April 24, 1891): Prussian General Field Marshal. As chief of the Prussian General Staff, he played a major role in Prussia's successes in the Wars of Unification. Moltke the Elder (his nickname was "the Great Silent One") was a student of Carl von Clausewitz and is considered the creator of a new, more modern method of leading armies in the field. Not only was he one of the most successful commanders of his time, but his concepts – not only in the military field – are still relevant today. Jack Welch developed his concept of "planned opportunism" on the basis of his studies of Moltke's work.

Müffling, Philipp Friedrich Carl Ferdinand von (* June 12, 1775; † January 16, 1851): Prussian General Field Marshal, geodesist and Chief of the Prussian General Staff.

Musashi, Miyamoto (* 1584; † June 13, 1645): Japanese Rōnin and founder of the Niten-Ichiryū school of swordsmanship; author of "Gorin no Sho" ("The Book of Five Rings"), which today serves primarily as a source of life wisdom and management strategies. Dokkodô ("The Lonely Way") contains 21 rules of self-discipline – given to Terao Magonojô on May 12, 1645. On May 19, 1645, Miyamoto Musashi died one week after the completion of his manuscript "The Book of Five Rings" in the cave Reigendô.

Nagelmackers, Georges (* June 24, 1845; † August 10, 1905): Belgian railroad entrepreneur and founder of the Compagnie Internationale des Wagons-Lits and the

Compagnie Internationale des Grands Hôtels; inventor of the Orient Express ("King of Trains" or "Train of Kings").

Net Present Value (NPV): accounting method for evaluating and comparing projects considering the time value of money.

$$\text{Net Present Value (NPV)} = \sum_{i=1}^{n} \frac{\text{Cash Flow in Year } i}{(1 + \text{Rate of Return})^i} - \text{Initial Investment } I_0$$

New Work: the concept of "New Work" was originally developed and introduced by the Austrian-American social philosopher Frithjof Bergmann in the late 1970s. His understanding of freedom is to "decide what you want to do because you believe in it". The central values of his concept are autonomy, freedom and participation in the community, creating space for creativity and self-actualization. The classic system of wage labor – according to Bergmann – is outdated and is being transformed into "New Work". New Work is based one-third on gainful employment, one-third on high-tech self-sufficiency ("high-tech self-providing") and "smart consumption", and one-third on "work that people really, really want". The somewhat vague, not uniformly defined term "new work" nowadays encompasses concepts of digital working, new work (time) models or creative workspaces, and is sometimes reduced to individual aspects of these.

Nonviolent Communication: communication approach based on the work of Marshall Rosenberg and principles of nonviolence by increasing empathy.

On War ("Vom Kriege"): the main theoretical work published only after the death of Carl von Clausewitz by his widow Marie von Clausewitz (1779–1836). Its theories of strategy, tactics and philosophy had a major influence on the development of modern warfare and are still taught today at military academies.

Operation Mincemeat: After the successful Allied landings in North Africa, British intelligence attempted to deceive Nazi Germany about the obvious next steps and plans: the invasion of Sicily. With "Operation Mincemeat", the German forces were fooled into believing an invasion of Sardinia and Greece. Reinforcements were therefore not sent to Sicily. The successful invasion of Sicily (i.e., "Operation Husky", 1943) was a crucial step in the Allied victory over Hitler and Mussolini.

Overtrading: usually occurs when companies expand too quickly. They are therefore very likely to experience liquidity problems and may run out of working capital (and could also run out of business).

Packard, David (* September 7, 1912; † March 26, 1996): U.S. entrepreneur and patron of the arts; co-founded the Hewlett-Packard technology company with Bill Hewlett.

Pareto principle: states that for many outcomes (e.g., success), roughly 80% of consequences (i.e., results) come from 20% of causes (e.g., efforts).

Patton, George Smith Jr. (* November 11, 1885; † December 21, 1945): U.S. general and military governor of Bavaria; commander of the Seventh United States Army in the Mediterranean Theater and the Third United States Army in France and Germany after the Allied invasion of Normandy in June 1944; philosophy of "leading from the front".

Pink, Daniel H.: non-fiction author and former speechwriter for U.S. Vice President Al Gore.

Porter, Michael: internationally known management expert, professor and author of "Competitive Strategy"; typical representative of the Design School.

Prahalad, Coimbatore Krishnarao (* August 8, 1941; † April 16, 2010): internationally known management professor, consultant, and author of "Competing for the future". Prahalad defined the concept of "Business Concept Innovation", "Resource leverage" and "Strategic stretch".

Process School (also Behavioral School): theory according to which strategy development is primarily a process. The representatives of this school emphasize the decision-making or incremental character of strategies.

Resource leverage: competitive strategy ("From Allocation to Leverage") according to Hamel and Prahalad; using the "leverage" of resources instead of pure resource allocation. As a result, even organizations with far fewer resources than the market leaders can win the competition: "management can leverage its resources, financial and nonfinancial, in five basic ways: by concentrating them more effectively on key strategic goals; by accumulating them more efficiently; by complementing one kind of resource with another to create higher order value; by conserving resources wherever possible; and by recovering them from the marketplace in the shortest possible time" (Hamel and Prahalad 1993).

Rosenberg, Marshall Bertram (* October 6, 1934; † February 7, 2015): American psychologist, mediator, author and teacher; developed the approach of "Nonviolent Communication".

Saint-Exupéry, Antoine de (* June 29, 1900; † July 31, 1944): French pilot and writer; creator of the "Little Prince", a plea for humanity and friendship. He is considered one of the best-known authors of the twentieth century.

Scharnhorst, Gerhard Johann David von (* November 12, 1755; † June 28, 1813): Prussian general and great reformer of the Prussian army during the Napoleonic Wars; first Chief of the Prussian General Staff and one of the protagonists in the victory over Napoleon.

Schwarzenegger, Arnold Alois (* July, 30 1947): Austrian-American, successful professional former body-builder, businessman, actor, and 38th governor of California.

SCRUM: Process model (lean development / project management), especially for agile software development.

Self-reflections (Meditations): the work of the Roman emperor Marcus Aurelius, written over a long period of time in Greek (probably in the 170s). The thoughts addressed to the author still belong to world literature. Gernot Krapinger writes: "Marcus Aurelius, the philosopher on the Roman imperial throne, recalled his role models and principles of life in the self-observations: reason-guided action, modesty, justice and humanity, self-discipline and inner serenity. He constantly reassured himself of his place in the world and tried to break through behavioral patterns through the power of his thoughts. Thus, he created timeless maxims for a mindful life".

Senger, Harro von: Swiss lawyer, sinologist, and professor emeritus; first Western expert on the Chinese "36 stratagems"; author of numerous works on the subject, such as "The Art of Cunning: Seeing Through and Applying Stratagems" and "36 Stratagems for Managers".

Serendipity: a chance observation of something not originally sought that turns out to be a new and surprising discovery ("opportunity"); term first used by British author Horace Walpole, fourth Earl of Orford (1717–1797). In a letter to his friend Horace Mann, Walpole refers to a Persian tale (The Three Princes of Serendip), Serendip being an old name for Ceylon (Sri Lanka) introduced by Arab traders. Harro von Senger calls the twelfth of the 36 stratagems "serendipity" or "kairos" stratagem.

Simplify your life: self-help book (first published in 2001) by Werner Tiki Küstenmacher and Lothar Seiwert on simplifying one's life with the topics of health, money, objects, spirituality and human relationships.

Six Sigma: method of quality management with statistical means for process improvement, which follows the procedure model "Define – Measure – Analyze – Improve – Control".

Stakeholder analysis (according to Grundy): to identify the different threats, main influence factors, and attitudes of different actors.

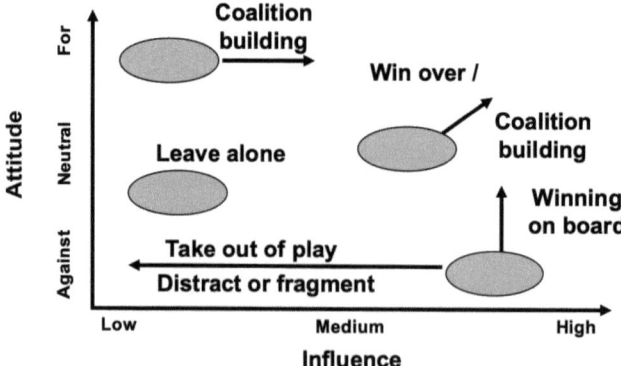

Figure: Stakeholder analysis according to Grundy

Stockdale, James Bond (* December 23, 1923; † July 5, 2005): vice admiral and one of the most highly decorated officers in the history of the United States Navy; taken as a prisoner of war in North Vietnam (1965–1973) during the Vietnam War. Management expert Jim Collins developed a leadership or motivational theory based on Stockdale's experiences, called the "Stockdale paradox", see also "Good to Great".

Strategic Balance Management:

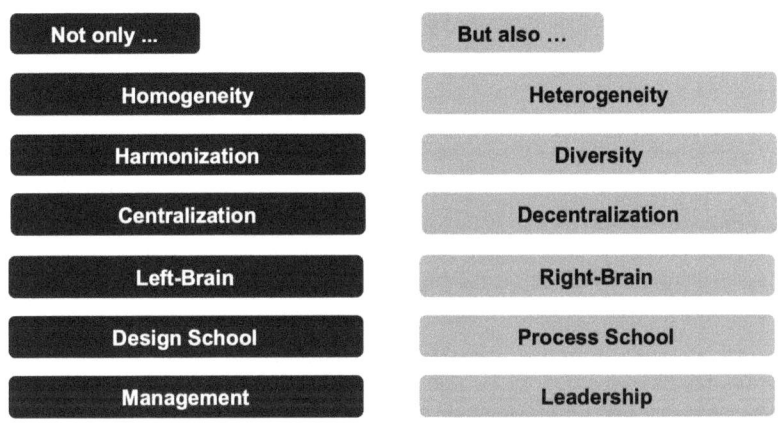

Figure: Find the right balance; it is not a comprehensive list (Ritter 2021)

Strategic Fit: expresses the extent to which an organization aligns its resources and capabilities with the opportunities of the external environment; in a broader sense, the congruence and "synchronization" of an organization's resources, capabilities, values, culture, goals and strategies.

Strategic Intent: in "Competing for the future", Hamel and Prahalad argue that most companies focus mainly on cost reduction instead of growth (e.g., new markets) and the future. They see this as a "lack of vision" and therefore suggest developing a vision and strategic intent that goes far beyond the present.

Strategic stretch: Hamel and Prahalad recommend in "Competing for the future" to achieve the strategic intent through "Resource leverage" and (temporary) "Strategic stretch" (i.e., extension/expansion) of the resources (similar to a sports team that surpasses and outgrows itself). In a nutshell: going the extra mile (cf. BHAG); but this only works for a limited time because of the risk of overstretching. Find the right balance.

Strategic Control Loop (according to Ritter): procedure model for the analysis and development of strategies in analogy to the analysis and design of control systems for dynamic (automated) systems.

Sunzi or Master Sun (* circa 544 B.C.; † circa 496 B.C.): Chinese general as well as outstanding military strategist and philosopher; author of the oldest and still important work on strategy: "The Art of War".

SWOT: acronym for Strengths, Weaknesses, Opportunities, and Threats; SWOT analysis is a tool for strategic analysis and planning in the positioning and strategy development of organizations.

The Art of War: the work of Master Sun (Sunzi), probably written around 500 B.C., is considered the earliest book and still one of the most important works on strategy ever written.

The Book of Five Rings ("Gorin no Sho"): the work of the Japanese Kensei ("Sword Saint") Miyamoto Musashi, written in the year of his death (1645), which serves primarily as a source of wisdom and management strategies.

The Dilbert Principle: a satirical management book (1997) by Scott Adams. According to the Dilbert Principle, in contrast to the Peter Principle, the most incompetent workers are systematically moved into management because they are perceived to do the least damage there.

The 15 Commitments of Conscious Leadership: A New Paradigm for Sustainable Success: book by Jim Dethmer, Diana Chapman and Kaley Warner Klemp on the leadership style they promote for sustainable success.

The Goal: a business novel (1984) by Eliyahu M. Goldratt discussing key elements of the "Theory of constraints". Time Magazine ranked the book among the "25 Most Influential Business Management Books".

The Thirty-Six Stratagems: a collection of stratagems (war lists) attributed to the Chinese general Tan Daoji († 436).

Total Quality Management (TQM): integrative management concept and holistic thinking for continuous improvement of quality and value creation.

Toyota Production System (TPS): the concept of a production system developed by Toyota based on lean management principles such as standardization, elimination of waste (the so-called seven wastes such as unnecessary rework, transportation, overproduction, ...), kanban, heijunka, continuous improvement (kaizen), just-in-time, takt time, and continuous flow.

Triple-S-Virtues for Success: management concept according to Arno and Roderick Ritter, based on 1) strategic thinking, 2) sense of serendipity, i.e., the development of a sensor for chances and opportunities (Pain & Gain) and the corresponding favorable timing (kairos) as well as 3) sense of serenity.

TUDAPOL Principle (according to Ritter): holistic principle for innovation, development and operation; based on innovation methods (Think Unlimited), agile principles (Develop Agile) and lean management (Produce and Operate Lean).

Value Stream Mapping: (graphical) method to analyze and define value streams

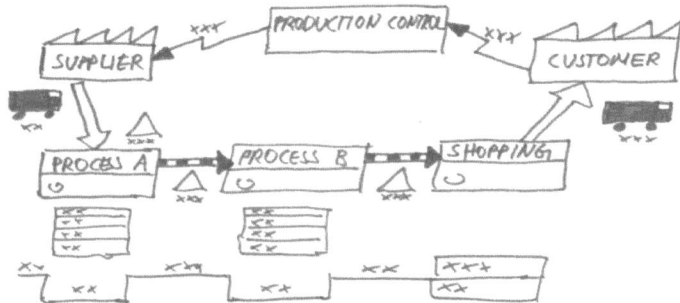

Figure: To analyze the AS-IS and to define the TO-BE by Value Stream Mapping, see Rother and Shook (2000), The Lean Enterprise Institute (2003) and Ritter (2020)

Wahnsinnskarriere ("Crazy career") — How careerists trick, what they sacrifice, how they rise: business novel (1999) by Wolfgang Schur and Günter Weick about the rise of careerists and opportunists.

Warnecke, Hans-Jürgen (* April 2, 1934; † March 19, 2019): professor of Industrial Manufacturing and Factory Operation at the University of Stuttgart and director of the Fraunhofer Institute for Manufacturing Engineering and Automation; President of the Fraunhofer-Gesellschaft from 1993 to 2002 and President of the Association of German Engineers (VDI) from 1995 to 1997.

Welch, John Francis Jr. (* November 19, 1935; † March 1, 2020): U.S. business executive, chemical engineer, Chairman and CEO of General Electric between 1981 and 2001.

Wright Brothers, i.e., Orville Wright (* August 19, 1871; † January 30, 1948) and Wilbur Wright (* April 16, 1867 — † May 30, 1912): American aviation pioneers, entrepreneurs and designers of the Wright Flyer, the world's first successful airplane (engine-powered, heavier-than-air aircraft); first successful flight with the Wright Flyer on December 17, 1903 (near Kitty Hawk, North Carolina).

Zero-defects production: error-free production (i.e., no rework) in the sense of kaizen or total quality management (TQM), based on the conviction that costs are incurred not only through quality, but also through the elimination of errors, which must be anticipated and eliminated as early as the development process.

References

Adams, D. (2000): Per Anhalter durch die Galaxis / The Hitchhiker's Guide to the Galaxy. 12th edition, Munich: Wilhelm Heyne Verlag (German edition)

Adams, S. (1998): Das Dilbert Prinzip / The Dilbert Principle. Munich: Wilhelm Heyne Verlag (German edition)

Allen, D. (2001): Getting Things Done: The Art of Stress-Free Productivity. Penguin Books

Balogun, J. and Hope Hailey, V. (2004): Exploring Strategic Change. 2nd edition, Harlow: FT Prentice Hall

Brown, S., Lamming, R., Bessant, J. and Jones, P. (2002): Strategic operations management. Oxford: Butterworth-Heinemann

Bryson, B. (2005): Eine kurze Geschichte von fast allem / A short history of nearly everything. 11th edition, Munich: Wilhelm Goldmann Verlag (German edition)

Clausewitz, C. von (2003): Vom Kriege / On War. Ernesto Grassi. 12th edition, Reinbek: Rowohlt (in German)

Collins, J. C. (2020): Der Weg zu den Besten. Die sieben Management-Prinzipien für dauerhaften Unternehmenserfolg / Good to Great: Why Some Companies Make the Leap and Others Don't. Frankfurt/New York: Campus Verlag (German edition)

Collins, J. C. and Porras, J. I. (2004): Built to Last: Successful Habits of Visionary Companies. 3rd edition, Harper Business

Covey, S. R. (2020): The 7 Habits of Highly Effective People. Powerful Lessons in Personal Change. 30th Anniversary Edition. London: Simon & Schuster

De Geus, A. (1988): Planning as Learning. Harvard Business Review, March 1988

Dethmer, J., Chapman, D. and Warner Klemp, K. (2015): The 15 Commitments of Conscious Leadership: A New Paradigm for Sustainable Success. 1st edition, Amazon Fulfillment

Drucker, P. (2014a): Was ist Management? Das Beste aus 50 Jahren / What is management? The best of 50 years. 7th edition, Econ (German edition)

Drucker, P. (2014b): The Effective Executive: Effektivität und Handlungsfähigkeit in der Führungsrolle gewinnen / The Effective Executive: Gaining Effectiveness and Ability to Act in the Leadership Role. 1st edition, München: Vahlen (German edition)

Föllinger, O. (1990): Regelungstechnik: Einführung in die Methoden und ihre Anwendung / Control engineering: introduction to the methods and their application. 6th, completely revised edition, Heidelberg: Hüthig (in German)

Frankl, V. (2019): Der Mensch vor der Frage nach dem Sinn / Man before the question of meaning. 30th edition, Munich: Piper (German edition)

Frankl, V. (2020): ... trotzdem Ja zum Leben sagen: Ein Psychologe erlebt das Konzentrationslager / Man's Search for Meaning. 10th edition, Penguin (German edition)

Franzke, J. (1998): Orient-Express, König der Züge / Orient-Express, King of the Trains. 1st edition, DB Museum (in German)

Freeman, E. (2019): DevOps For Dummies. 1st edition, John Willey & Sons

Goldratt, E. (2001): Das Ziel / The Goal. Excellence in Manufacturing. Frankfurt/Main: Campus Verlag (German edition)

Grant, M. R. (2002): Contemporary strategy analysis – concepts, techniques, applications. 4th edition, Blackwell publishing

Grichnik, D., Brettel, M., Koropp, C. and Mauer, R. (2017): Entrepreneurship. Unternehmerisches Denken, Entscheiden und Handeln in innovativen und technologie-orientierten Unternehmungen / Entrepreneurship. Entrepreneurial thinking, decision-making and action in innovative and technology-oriented companies. 2nd edition, Schäfer-Poeschel (in German)

Grimmelshausen, H. J. von (1986): Der abenteuerliche Simplicissimus Teutsch / Simplicius Simplicissimus. Afterword by Volker Meid. Reclam (in German)

Hackl, B., Wagner, M., Attmer, L. and Baumann, D. (2017): New Work: Auf dem Weg zur neuen Arbeitswelt. Management-Impulse, Praxisbeispiele, Studien / New Work: On the way to the new working world. Management impulses, practical examples, studies. Springer Gabler (in German)

Hamel, G. (2002): Leading the Revolution – How to Thrive in Turbulent Times by Making Innovation a Way of Life. New York: Plume

Hamel, G. and Prahalad, C. K. (1993): Strategy as Stretch and Leverage. Harvard Business Review, March-April 1993

Hamel, G. and Prahalad, C. K. (1997): Wettlauf um die Zukunft / Competing for the future. Vienna: Wirtschaftsverlag Ueberreuter (German edition)

Harari, Y. N. (2015): Eine kurze Geschichte der Menschheit / A brief history of humankind. 17th edition, Pantheon (German edition)

Harari, Y. N. (2019): Homo Deus. Eine Geschichte von Morgen / Homo Deus. A Brief History of Tomorrow. 6th edition, C.H. Beck (German edition)

Hendricks, G. (2009): THE BIG LEAP: Conquer Your Hidden Fear and Take Life to the Next Level. HarperOne

Hoffmeister, C. (2015): Digital Business Modelling – Digitale Geschäftsmodelle entwickeln und strategisch verankern / Digital Business Modeling – Developing and strategically anchoring digital business models. 1st edition, Hanser (in German)

Jobber, D. (2001): Principles & Practice of Marketing. 3rd edition, McGraw-Hill

Khalsa, M. (1999): Let's Get Real or Let's Not Play: The Demise of Dysfunctional Selling and the Advent of Helping Clients Succeed. Franklin Covey

Küstenmacher, W. T. and Seiwert, L. (2003): simplify your life: Einfacher und glücklicher leben / simplify your life: live more simply and happily. 10th edition. Campus Verlag Frankfurt (German edition)

Kutschker, M. and Schmid, S. (2011): Internationales Management / International Management. 7th edition, Munich: Oldenbourg Verlag (in German)

Limoncelli, T., Chalup, S. and Hogan, C. (2015): The practice of cloud system administration. Designing and operating large distributed systems. Vol. 2, Addison-Wesley

Machiavelli, N. (2001): Der Fürst – Il Principe / The Prince. 1st edition, Frankfurt am Main: Insel Verlag (German edition)

Machiavelli, N. (2021): Discorsi – Staat und Politik / Discorsi – State and Politics. 7th edition, Frankfurt am Main: Insel Verlag (German edition)

Mackenzie, A. (1997): The Time Trap: The Classic Book on Time Management. 3rd edition, AMACOM

Marc Aurel (2019): Selbstbetrachtungen (Self-Reflections) / Meditations. 1st edition, Reclam (German edition)

Mell, H. (2023): Die zehn wichtigsten "systemimmanenten" Grundregeln für den Erfolg im Beruf / The ten most important "system-immanent" basic rules for success at work. VDI nachrichten. 10th of February 2023 / Vol. 3, pages 36-37 (in German)

Mintzberg, H. and Lampel, J. (1999): Reflecting on the Strategy Process. Sloan Management Review

Mintzberg, H., Quinn, J. B. and Ghoshal, S. (1998): The Strategy Process. Revised European Edition, Harlow: FT Prentice Hall

Mintzberg, H. and Westley, F. (2001): Decision Making: It's Not What You Think. Sloan Management Review, pages 89-93

Möbius, I. and Bigge, W. (2023): Generalfeldmarschall Graf Moltke: Ein militärisches Lebensbild / Field Marshal Count Moltke: A Military Portrait of his Life. Edited & Reprint (1901), Chemnitz: Eigenverlag Ingo Möbius (in German)

Moltke, H. Graf von (2017): Moltkes militärische Werke / Moltke's military works. Reprint (1892), hansebook (in German)

Mullins, L. J. (2002): Management and organisational behaviour. 6th edition, Harlow: FT Prentice Hall

Musashi, M. (2021): Das Buch der fünf Ringe: Klassische Strategien aus dem alten Japan / The Book of Five Rings: Classical Strategies from Ancient Japan. 5th edition, Munich: Piper (German edition)

Nagler, J. (2015): Abraham Lincoln – Amerikas großer Präsident / Abraham Lincoln – America's Great President. 3rd edition, Munich: C.H.Beck (in German)

Neale, B. and McElroy, T. (2004): Business Finance – A Value-Based Approach. 1st edition, Harlow: FT Prentice Hall

Ohmae, K. (1985): The mind of the strategist – business planning for competitive advantage. Harmondsworth: Penguin

Osterwalder, A. and Pigneur, Y. (2011): Business Model Generation: Ein Handbuch für Visionäre, Spielveränderer und Herausforderer / Business Model Generation: A Handbook for Visionaries, Game Changers, and Challengers. 1st edition, Campus-Verlag (German edition)

Pink, D. (2008): A Whole New Mind – Why Right-Brainers Will Rule the Future. Marshal Cavendish Limited

Pfeifer, T. (1993): Qualitätsmanagement – Strategien, Methoden / Quality Management – strategies, methods. Munich: Hanser (in German)

Porter, M. E. (1999): Wettbewerbsstrategie / Competitive Strategy. 10th edition, Frankfurt: Campus Verlag Frankfurt (German edition)

Preußig, J. (2015): Agiles Projektmanagement / Agile project management. Scrum, Use Cases, Task Boards & Co. 1st edition, Haufe Lexware (in German)

Ritter, A. (2013): Strategisches Management: Von der Theorie zur Implementierung / Strategic Management: from theory to implementation. Management-Kompass. 1st edition, Norderstedt: BoD Books on Demand (in German)

Ritter, A. (2019): 50 Wege im Management Erfolg zu verhindern / 50 Ways within management to prevent success. Management-Kompass. 1st edition, Norderstedt: BoD Books on Demand (in German)

Ritter, A. (2020): The TUDAPOL Principle: The way to think unlimited, develop agile, produce & operate lean. Management-Compass. 1st edition, Norderstedt: BoD Books on Demand

Ritter, A. (2021): The BANWAD WAY: Beyond Agile, New Work and Digitalization. Management-Compass. 1st edition, Norderstedt: BoD Books on Demand

Ritter, A. and Ritter R. (2022): Auf der Suche nach dem Geheimnis unseres Erfolges: Eine Analyse und Business-Novelle / In search of the secret of our success: An analysis and business novel. Management-Kompass. Norderstedt: BoD Books on Demand (in German)

Rosenberg, M. (2012): Konflikte lösen durch Gewaltfreie Kommunikation / Solving conflicts through nonviolent communication. 15th edition, Freiburg: Herder (in German)

Rother, M. and Shook, J. (2000): Sehen lernen / Learning to See – Value Stream Mapping to Add Value and Eliminate Muda. Log_X (German edition)

Roxburgh, C. (2003): Hidden flaws in strategy. The McKinsey Quarterly 2003 Number 2. Pages 27-39

Schur, W. and Weick, G. (2005): Wahnsinnskarriere / Crazy career – Wie Karrieremacher tricksen, was sie opfern, wie sie aufsteigen / How careerists trick, what they sacrifice, how they rise. 2nd edition, Frankfurt: Eichborn (in German)

Senger, H. von (2016): Die Kunst der List: Strategeme durchschauen und anwenden / The art of cunning: seeing through and applying stratagems. 6th, revised edition, Munich: C.H.Beck (German edition)

Senger, H. von (2016): 36 Strategeme für Manager / 36 stratagems for managers. 5th, revised edition, Carl Hanser Verlag (German edition)

Simonyi, K. (1995): Kulturgeschichte der Physik. Von den Anfängen bis 1990 / Cultural history of physics. From the beginnings to 1990. 2nd edition, Verlag Harri Deutsch. Thun / Frankfurt am Main (German edition)

Sunzi (2001): Die Kunst des Krieges / The art of war. Knaur – Claussen & Bosse (German edition)

The Lean Enterprise Institute (2003): Lean Lexicon – A graphical glossary for Lean Thinkers. The Lean Enterprise Institute, Brookline, Massachusetts, USA

Vahs, D. and Brem, A. (2015): Innovationsmanagement. Von der Idee zur erfolgreichen Vermarktung / Innovation management. From the idea to successful marketing. 5th edition, Schäffer-Poeschel (in German)

Warnecke, H.-J. (1999): Projekt Zukunft – Die Megatrends in Wissenschaft und Technik / Project Future – Megatrends in science and technology. Cologne: vgs Köln (in German)

Westkämper, E. (1997): Null-Fehler-Produktion in Prozeßketten / Zero-defects production. Heidelberg: Springer (in German)

Westkämper, E. (1999): Die Wandlungsfähigkeit von Unternehmen / The transformability of enterprises. wt Werkstattstechnik, vol. 89 / 4 (in German)

Movie and Song Directory

Burns, K. (1990): The Civil War. American television documentary miniseries, Public Broadcasting Service

Burns, K. und Novick, L. (2007): The War. American television documentary miniseries, Public Broadcasting Service

Burns, K. and Novick, L. (2017): The Vietnam War. American television documentary miniseries, Public Broadcasting Service

Chilcott, L. (2023): Arnold. Documentary miniseries, Netflix

Ficarra, G. and Requa, J. (2011): Crazy, Stupid, Love. American romantic comedy film, Warner Bros. Pictures

Hancock, J. L. (2016): The Founder. American biographical drama film, The Weinstein Company

Huntgeburth, H. (2020): Lindenberg! Mach dein Ding / Lindenberg! Do your thing. Feature film about the beginning of Udo Lindenberg's music career with flashbacks to his childhood and youth, Letterbox Filmproduktion

Judge, M. (1999): Office Space. American black comedy film, 20th Century Fox

Käutner, H. (1956): Der Hauptmann von Köpenick / The Captain of Köpenick. Drama, Real-Film

Lindenberg, U. (2019): Niemals dran gezweifelt / Never doubted it. Single (Album)

Madden, J. (2022): Operation Mincemeat. British war drama film, Warner Bros. Pictures / Netflix

Mangold, J. (2010): Knight and Day. American action-comedy film, 20th Century Fox

McGuigan, P. (2006): Lucky Number Slevin. Neo-noir crime thriller film, Metro-Goldwyn-Mayer

McKay, A. (2015): The Big Short. Biographical comedy-drama, Paramount Pictures

Rockaway, E. (2021): Lansky. American biographical crime drama, Vertical Entertainment

Ross, H. (1987): The Secret of My Succe$s. Comedy Film, Universal Pictures

Scott, R. (2001): Black Hawk Down. War-drama, Columbia Pictures

Shore, D. and Cranston, B. (2015–2019): Sneaky Pete. Crime drama series, Amazon Prime Video

Soderbergh, S. (2017): Logan Lucky. Heist comedy film, Fingerprint Releasing / Bleecker Street

Whedon, J. (2002): Firefly. American space Western drama television series, Fox

Whedon, J. (2005): Serenity. American space Western film, based on Firefly, Universal Pictures

Woo, J. (2008–2009): Red Cliff. Chinese epic war film, Summit Entertainment

Internet Link Directory

Everything must be made as simple as possible. But not simpler:
https://quoteinvestigator.com/2011/05/13/einstein-simple/ (Status: August 2024)

He who stops getting better has stopped being good:
https://quoteinvestigator.com/2019/10/27/good-better/ (Status: August 2024)

It is not the most intellectual of the species that survives; it is not the strongest that survives; but the species that survives is the one that is able best to adapt and adjust to the changing environment in which it finds itself:
https://quoteinvestigator.com/2014/05/04/adapt/ (Status: August 2024)

Jim Collins:
https://www.jimcollins.com/ (Status: August 2024)

Matthew 10:16 (New International Version)**:**
https://www.biblegateway.com/passage/?search=Matthew%2010%3A16&version=NIV
(Status: August 2024)

Mein Leben ist ein Kampf:
https://beruhmte-zitate.de/zitate/125817-voltaire-mein-leben-ist-ein-kampf/ (Status:
August 2024)

Never take counsel of your fears:
https://beruhmte-zitate.de/zitate/131170-andrew-jackson-angst-ist-ein-schlechter-
ratgeber/ (Status: August 2024)

Plans are worthless, but planning is everything:
https://quoteinvestigator.com/2017/11/18/planning/ Status: August 2024)

**Solowjow, D. (2009): Kalashnikov, 90, decries "criminal" use of rifle. In:
Reuters. October 26, 2009:**
https://www.reuters.com/article/idUSLQ148454 (Status: August 2024)

Success:
https://www.oxfordlearnersdictionaries.com/definition/english/success (Status: August
2024)

Success:
https://en.wikipedia.org/wiki/Success_(concept) (Status: August 2024)

Success Is Never Final and Failure Never Fatal. It's Courage That Counts:
https://quoteinvestigator.com/2013/09/03/success-final/ (Status: August 2024)

Theory of constraint:
https://en.wikipedia.org/wiki/Theory_of_constraints (Status: August 2024).

Wie Pech und Schwefel:
https://de.wikipedia.org/wiki/Fallschirmjägerbataillon_261 (Status: August 2024)

Space for Notes

Published by the Authors at BoD

Strategisches Management: Von der Theorie zur Implementierung: Management-Kompass
ISBN-10: 3848229234 and ISBN-13: 978-3848229239

50 Wege im Management Erfolg zu verhindern: Management-Kompass
ISBN-10: 3741294837 and ISBN-13: 978-3741294839

The Consultant: Einsatz wider Willen
ISBN-10: 374129490X and ISBN-13: 978-3741294907

The TUDAPOL Principle: The Way to Think Unlimited, Develop Agile, Produce & Operate Lean
ISBN-10: 3751915273 and ISBN-13: 978-3751915274

The Consultant: Agile versus Safe
ISBN-10: 3751997210 and ISBN-13: 978-3751997218

The BANWAD Way: Beyond Agile, New Work and Digitalization: Management-Compass
ISBN-10: 3752689447 and ISBN-13: 978-3752689440

Auf der Suche nach dem Geheimnis unseres Erfolges: Eine Analyse und Business-Novelle
ISBN-10: 3756836630 and ISBN-13: 978-3756836635